Successful Product Design

Dedications

To my wife, Gill, who probably knows as much about design management now as any of us   (B.H.)

To all those engineers who have contributed to exciting projects that have failed on the market   (S.P.)

Thanks to Benn Harrison for his cartoons

Successful Product Design

What to do and when

Bill Hollins BSc(Hons), MBIM
Senior Lecturer, London Management Centre, Polytechnic of Central London

Stuart Pugh BSc(Eng), CEng, FIMechE, FRSA, REngDes
Babcock Professor of Engineering Design, University of Strathclyde

Butterworths
London   Boston   Singapore   Sydney   Toronto   Wellington

 PART OF REED INTERNATIONAL P.L.C.

First published 1990

© Butterworth & Co. (Publishers) Ltd, 1990

British Library Cataloguing in Publication Data

Hollins, Bill
  Successful product design
  1. Products. Design
  I. Title II. Pugh, Stuart
  658.5'752
  ISBN 0–408–03861–6

Library of Congress Cataloging-in-Publication Data

Hollins, Bill
  Successful product design: what to do and when/Bill
  Hollins, Stuart Pugh.
    p. cm.
  Includes bibliographical references.
  ISBN 0–408–03861–6
    1. Design, Industrial—Management. I. Pugh,
Stuart. II. Title.
TS171.4.H65   1989
658.5'752—dc20   89–38948

Phototypeset by Scribe Design, Gillingham, Kent
Printed and bound in Great Britain by Butler & Tanner,
Frome, Somerset

Foreword

With increasing global competition from the Far East, the Western world is perhaps at last taking seriously the concept of world markets for its products. Central to this process of recognition is the fact that our processes of design leave much to be desired in meeting this competition, and, perhaps more to the point in the context of this book, that a necessary redefinition of 'design' is essential to meet these challenges. In other words, a 'total design' approach is required, however that may be defined.

There is considerable evidence of the adoption of the total approach by companies in the USA and the UK, and it is well known that some of the US giants such as Xerox, General Motors and Ford are giving urgent attention to processes other than those of production. This shows a foresight based presumably on fear; whatever the stimulus, the fact that companies have at last recognized a need for more systematic, rigorous and sophisticated design processes is a step not only in the right direction but one towards survival.

Writing this book represents but another step in that direction, and was based on the recognition – now axiomatic, it is to be hoped – that unless 'front end' design processes were better understood and defined, leading to more certainty of success, then subsequent company activities such as engineering, development, trials and financial planning would be a waste of time and money. This is borne out by the high incidence of new product failures. It is to the issues at the front end of the process of 'total design' that our research and subsequent book have been addressed.

This book has a carefully chosen title, since success and how to achieve it is its central theme, and, we hope, represents yet another step forward in systematic competitive design. We and our trial industries know it works, and we hope that it will motivate your company to compete effectively.

One word of caution: what is recommended here is not a mechanistic, fruit-machine type of process – i.e. pulling the handle and hoping to win the jackpot. We have provided the route and amplified the directions. It is up to the people involved in the design team to travel that route. Ultimately it is the quality of their actions within the framework provided that will lead to success.

Stuart Pugh

Preface

After twenty years in engineering and sixteen years designing products in industry, most of that time at a management level, I had come to the conclusion that I still did not know how to organize the design process. It generally appeared to be clear what should be done at the detailing stage and beyond, and, although mistakes were made, there were many books telling readers what should be done and how it should be done once this stage had been reached. It was the part before this, the 'front end' of design, that caused confusion.

It was a problem not just for me, but for many other design managers. We generally agreed that information should be presented as a product design specification (or a similar form under another name), and that this should be a detailed document originating from the marketing department, covering all aspects of the product to be designed. However, a product design specification involved a great deal of work, and this might be completed only for it to be found that, for one reason of another, the product was unsuitable for the company or for the market, so that the design was quickly abandoned. The result was that most marketing managers supplied the design department with a hastily formulated specification or product brief on which design and often detailing would start, only to revise it heavily when better market information became known; but by this time the product might well be approaching, or even in, production.

I realized that what was required was a more progressive approach to the design process; one that would avoid the necessity for a fully developed product design specification until it was certain that it was needed and, preferably, would eliminate unsuitable design projects before the product design specification was written.

At that time I was Design Director in a company manufacturing safety equipment. One day, the Technical Director said to me, holding up one of the company's products, 'This product has been good for the past fifty years and I reckon it will be good for the next fifty.' I felt this was wrong, and as a designer it was in my interests to believe that he was wrong, but I had no way of proving or disproving his statement. This led me to consider whether there were some products that, perhaps, did not require any redesign or further design at all, or others that did require design but only in certain areas – but which areas?

Shortly after this I left the company and met Stuart Pugh, who seemed to be one of the very few people who shared the view that the major difficulties in design and its management originated from the front end: that is, from the market need or product idea through to the detailing stage.

From early in 1985 we have been researching this particular area of design, initially at the Engineering Design Centre at Loughborough University of

Technology and, latterly, in the Design Division at the University of Strathclyde. All the research was undertaken within industry and for industry. One of the outcomes is this book.

The structure of the book

In Part 1 the scene is set for an improved design process with an explanation of product status, why such a design process is required and where design management should be emphasized.

Part 2 is the most important section. It describes the improved design process in its layered form supplemented by a support text that gives justification or clarification of the recommendations for action made in the process layers.

Part 3 shows a worked example of the system product – a paper clip – in a fictional company. Also in this part is an example of the need for product definition. The work that led to this book is briefly outlined in the Appendix.

After each section of the design process there is a *support text* which provides the reference to, or the reasoning behind, the choice and sequence of the activities that make up the design process. These are referred to in main text by 'ST', followed by a number which relates to the relevant section of the support text. Note that it is not necessary to read the support text to use this design process.

Data have been obtained from two sources. Previous research by others has been investigated and, where worthwhile or helpful, has been included. Our own research has produced findings that justify many of the statements made, especially in the area of finding the product status.

Bill Hollins

Contents

Foreword   v
Preface   vii
Definitions   xiii

Part 1

1 The need for the process of total design   3

2 The format of this book   5
2.1 Limitations in the scope of this book   5
2.2 The management of product design   6
2.3 The link with marketing   7

3 The need for good design management   9
3.1 The importance of effective product design management   9
3.2 Success and failure of product design   10
3.3 The low-cost end of design   12

4 Successful design through product status   17
4.1 What is product status?   17
4.2 The need to look for product status   20
4.3 The advantage of knowing the product status   23
4.4 Factors that make a product static or dynamic   24
4.5 Product status in the development of a typical product   36
4.6 Product status related to the product life cycle and the S-shaped curve   38
4.7 Product status as a method for forecasting and prediction   42
4.8 Do you already know your product's status?   43

Part 2

5 The improved process of total design   47
5.1 Introduction to the total design process   47
5.2 Overall presentation of the total design plan   48
5.3 The design activity model   48
5.4 The design team   52
5.5 Project documentation   55

5.6 Marketing and the design plan   55
5.7 The quantity dilemma   56

INTRODUCTION SUPPORT TEXT
I.1 The most efficient presentation of the design plan   58
I.2 Design reviews   59
I.3 Product status in relation to the design activity model   60
I.4 Organic and mechanistic structures   61
I.5 Communication   62
I.6 Product champions   63

6 A system for total design management of products   64

Preliminary Layer: Before design begins   64
PRELIMINARY LAYER SUPPORT TEXT
PL1 Management commitment   65
PL2 Financial control   66

Layer 1: Product definition   68
LAYER 1 SUPPORT TEXT
L1.1 Sources for new product design   69
L1.2 Market pull   70
L1.3 Technology push   70

Layer 2: Status specification   72
Type of information needed and possible sources   73

LAYER 2 SUPPORT TEXT
L2.1 Market research and product status   73
L2.2 Innovation seeking outside industry   75

Layer 3: Ascertain product status   79
The status questionnaires   79
LAYER 3 SUPPORT TEXT
L3.1 The advantages of using the questionnaires   80
L3.2 Periodic check on product status   81
L3.3 Company size and product status   81

Layer 4A: Write the product design specfication   84
LAYER 4A SUPPORT TEXT
L4A.1 The product design specification   86
L4A.2 The contents of the product design specification   87
L4A.3 Product status in relation to the product design specification   97
L4A.4 Parametric analysis   98
L4A.5 Grading the elements of the product design specification   102
L4A.6 Product disposal   105

Layer 4B: Relate design disciplines to the product status   108
A dynamic product   108
A static product   110
LAYER 4B SUPPORT TEXT
L4B.1   The importance of production volume as opposed to time in production and the design plan   112
L4B.2   Non-product-related research   113
L4B.3   Customer training   113
L4B.4   Subcontract manufacture   113
L4B.5   Patents and design protection   114
L4B.6   Low-cost production   114
L4B.7   Aesthetics and fashion in design   115
L4B.8   Finish   115
L4B.9   Ergonomics and maintainability   115
L4B.10 Size reduction   116

L4B.11 Business planning   116
L4B.12 Use of reputation   116
L4B.13 Use of standards in design   117
L4B.14 Fast delivery, effective distribution   117
L4B.15 After-sales service   117
L4B.16 Imitation and imitators   118
L4B.17 Group technology   118
L4B.18 CAD and CAM   119
L4B.19 The change of emphasis from product design to process design   119
L4B.20 The use of different materials in design   121

Layer 5: Static 2 disciplines   122
Static 2 products   122

LAYER 5 SUPPORT TEXT
L5.1   Niche marketing   124
L5.2   Rationalization   125
L5.3   Economies of scale   125
L5.4   Automation   126
L5.5   Worker specialization   126
L5.6   Energy conservation   127
L5.7   Just in time (Kanban)   127
L5.8   Value analysis   128
L5.9   Sensitivity analysis   129
L5.10 The importance of market share   129
L5.11 Expert systems   129

Part 3

7 A worked example of the system   135

8 An example of the need for the product definition   153

Appendix The research that led to this book   159

References   161

Index   165

Definitions

The following definitions are used throughout this book, and should be assimilated before the design system can be used effectively.

Business plan   Overall aims of an organization in whatever terms are appropriate (e.g. financial, social, ecological).

Conceptually vulnerable design   Where a product is treated as static when it is potentially dynamic, or the concept chosen is under threat from a 'better' product concept (such as an innovation) or when the wrong concept is chosen. (First used in Pugh, 1981.)

Conformance standard   A requirement by law, a standards institute or an insurance company.

Design disciplines   Throughout this book various techniques that accompany design have been identified that are of benefit to the organization and process of design. There is no one word that accurately describes all these packages of techniques, but that chosen and used throughout this book is 'discipline', the dictionary definition of which includes 'system, rule, method and arrangement'. Therefore although certain activities cannot strictly be termed disciplines (e.g. financial control, seeking innovations outside industry and emphasizing market-pull products) these and other activities are referred to under the heading 'Design disciplines'.

Design efficiency   The formula for this is:

$$\frac{\text{quality of design}}{\text{total cost of design}}$$

Design model   A diagram showing the general procedure for the design of a product or service.

Design plan   A 'route map' to guide the user through the design process.

Design review   A formal, documented, comprehensive and systematic examination of the capability of a design to meet the product design specification, to identify problems and propose solutions. Design reviews should be held when necessary and must involve all who can make a contribution.

Dynamic company   A company that has the attributes associated with the design and/or production of a dynamic product.

Dynamic product   A product where design changes are (or should be) innovative. The concept is likely to change.

Elements of the product design specification   The areas of investigation that are included in the product design specification.

Evolutionary design   Continuous product improvement to meet slowly changing market needs or evolving science and technology aimed at sustaining or expanding existing markets (Parker, 1980).

Front end of design   That part of the design process that precedes the detail design stage.

Imitator   A company that copies the design of another company's product (sometimes known as 'me too' type products).

Innovation   The process of taking an invention forward into the first marketable product.

Invention   The act of insight by which a new and promising technical possibility is recognized and worked out (at least mentally and perhaps physically) in its essential, most rudimentary form (Schener, 1971).

Management of product design   The planning, organization and control of money, men, materials and time to achieve the objectives of the project (SEED, 1985).

Marketing   The management function responsible for identifying, anticipating and satisfying customer requirements profitably (The Institute of Marketing).

Partial design   Part of the design which contributes to the whole (e.g. industrial design, engineering design, design for manufacture, etc.).

Partial product design specification   A full, written document that covers the relevant aspects of the product from which part of the product should be designed.

Performance function   An overall measure of all aspects of a product which allows it to be compared with another, similar, product.

Process design   Design of the method of manufacture.

Product/company status mismatch   When a company is structured for or is treating a product as static and the product is dynamic. Conversely, when a company that is structured for or is treating a product as dynamic and the product is static.

Product design specification   A definitive document specifying the requirements to which the resulting product should conform.

Product failure   A product failing to live up to its company's expectations in the market (Foxall, 1984).

Product standard   A standard that customers are used to, prefer or may require to fit or interface with their existing products.

Product status   The term used to describe whether the overall conceptual design of a product is truly static, temporarily static or dynamic, i.e. likely to change or need changing (Pugh, 1981).

Reliability   The ability of an item to perform a required function under stated conditions for a given period of time (ISO 8402: 1986).

Standard design   A product design that fixes the concept for a period of time. It fulfils the market requirements more closely than other designs available at that time and sets the static plateau.

Static 1   The static design disciplines that are necessary to enable a product to be produced competitively.

Static 2   The static design disciplines that can be introduced when the production volume reaches a level that makes their inclusion viable.

Static company   A company that has the attributes associated with the design and/or production of a static product.

Static product   A product where design changes are (or should be) incremental or non-existent. The concept is unlikely to change.

Total design   A multidisciplinary iterative process that takes an idea or market need forward into a successful product (see the Design Activity Model, Part 2, Introduction). (*Note*: Design does not end with production, but with product disposal.)

Part 1

For the foresight of things to come, which is providence, belongs only to him by whose will they are to come. From him only, and supernaturally, proceeds prophecy. The best prophet naturally is the best guesser, he that is most versed and studied in the matters he guesses at; for he hath the most signs to guess by.

Thomas Hobbes, *The Leviathan* (1651)

1 The need for the process of total design

Many engineers in all disciplines are researching the design process – usually from an 'engineering design' point of view. Since this research is mainly into existing practice, this has resulted in erudite papers and books which add to the diagnostic stock but give little guidance on curing the diseases. In parallel we have the business school approach which, until recently, took the product in a business as 'given'. Business schools also research the causes of business failure, the results being remarkably akin to those of engineering design research: heavy in diagnosis, light on cure – except through exhortation.

Cooper (1983), having investigated various studies on new product success and failure, states: 'What is missing is a shaping of the research conclusions into a managerial guide.' He later outlines the requirements for an ideal process model for industrial products, and the process given in this book fulfils them all (Part 2).

In adopting a strategy based upon *total design* (defined as the systematic activity necessary from the identification of a market of user need to the selling of the successful product to satisfy that need) this book attempts to reconcile the parallel schools of research into one having a common focus – the product. Since the successful engineering of a product for a non-receptive market would be construed as failure, so would a badly engineered product for a receptive market.

Our view of total design is characterized by clear definition, a feature notably lacking in many publications worldwide. Total design may be equated with the *new product development process* of Professor Don Clausing of MIT, who, as recently as 1986, said: 'Despite the importance of the product development process, it has received little attention, as a structured systematic process.' Perhaps this book goes some way towards resolving this issue.

Hales (1987) observes that this situation has not changed:

In review it appears that:
(i) Despite a long history of innovative engineering design in industry and development of many prescriptive methods and models, the engineering design process is not yet considered well understood or adequately exploited in practice.
(ii) There is a mismatch between the design process as it is currently modelled in theory and what actually happens in practice.
(iii) There is strong support for research aimed at developing a basic understanding of the engineering design process and improving the effectiveness in practice (p. 12).

Others refer to total design differently and, as a result, where definitions do exist, they are either partial, unclear or both. Two quotations summarize the thinking behind this book:

Design is concerned with making things people want (Gregory, 1966).

Production is sales is design is marketing (Heller, 1984).

This book is about how to do it, how to carry out successful product design in a total sense. If you think that the product strategy is obvious then you probably know a lot about design and how difficult it is to achieve success in today's markets. If you think it is both obvious and easy then you probably know very little about design in the modern sense of the word, i.e. *total*.

2 The format of this book

2.1 Limitations in the scope of this book

The original research that led to the compilation of this book initially was directed towards the management of the design of manufactured mechanical products. However, it became apparent, as the work progressed, that the concepts were applicable to a much wider area of product design. These concepts were tested in companies outside the area of mechanical engineering and were still found to hold good. It is, therefore, believed that the basic principles incorporated into this book hold good for all products, although, for service industries and architecture, it would need significant adaption in content but not in sequence.

Although the main purpose of the book is to give guidance in design management mainly at the early stages or 'front end' of design (i.e. the part of design from the market research input to the start of detail design), where the previously unexplained and little-researched problem area of design is known to exist, this area cannot be taken entirely in isolation. Therefore recommendations are also made in respect of market research, marketing and aspects of manufacture. Consideration has not been given as to how new concepts are generated or how to judge their worth, beyond statements as to whether they should be considered and how they should be viewed in relation to existing products. It is now almost universally accepted that the compilation of the product design specification (often known by other names) is the most important part of the design process, and this has been assumed to be correct in this book.

The area of product design is subject to many influences. A perfectly engineered product will fail if the market research identified the wrong market or the market changed, production did not make the product correctly, distribution and marketing were poor or that the company decided not to proceed with the product for one reason or another. Attempts have been made to identify these areas in this book.

The authors believe that design without products is a somewhat sterile activity. The purpose of design is to provide a product that fulfils a market need and, therefore, the product is central to this design guide. Much has been written about design and its management that overlooks the importance of products, occasionally even to the exclusion of their mention. Other writers have been more forthright on the subject. Gregory (1985) stated:

> Since the product is the focus of business strategy it is, of necessity, 'the valued object' towards which the design is directed. It is necessary, once more, to set the valued object and its conceptual precursors at the centre of design concern.

Deasley (1986) also confirms its importance: 'Central to any business are its products: they generate wealth, and differentiate a company from its competitors.' Throughout this book the product and its status has been the central focus.

2.2 The management of product design

Many people have stated that there needs to be a greater understanding of the process of product design. We believe that what we offer goes some way towards fulfilling these needs, and this has been confirmed by design managers employed in industry.

To our knowledge, before this book, there was no means of identifying whether a product was static or dynamic (or other terms describing innovation or incremental change). This is now possible by using the status questionnaires. Even if someone knew their product status, there was no method for determining when this was likely to change from static to dynamic or dynamic to static. It is necessary to know this in order to direct a design team effectively. For example, we may be called upon to innovate more, but there are times when products should not be innovated. As innovation is both expensive and time consuming, knowing when it is necessary and when it can be avoided has obvious advantages to design managers. Sometimes it is better to concentrate on static design. We will also show whether a company is better structured to undertake static or dynamic design.

Having detemined the status of the company's products, a design manager then needs a comprehensive list of disciplines to use when a product is being designed. Such a list has been compiled from research and is included in this book.

Without first defining whether a product design was static or dynamic a design manager would have to assume that all the disciplines were important all the time. The design process shows which disciplines should be emphasized and which are of less importance by relating them to product status. This means that design effort can be reduced.

Even with a comprehensive list of disciplines, the design team needs to know *when* they should be used. The main part of this book is a design process that leads the user through the various stages of product design. This is accompanied by reasons for or justifications of each recommended course of action. There is also a worked example of the design process to help further with the understanding of the system's use.

The main decisions taken in the design of products (and the major mistakes) occur in the early stages of the design process. It is at the front end of design where the design manager and the design team need to concentrate their effort. The reader will discover that this front-end bias is emphasized in this book.

Product status, as a guide to the treatment of product design, can be used as an aid to forecasting and product planning. Also, it is shown that it is possible to rank the elements in the product design specfication for importance, although reliability is confirmed as being the single most important aspect of design. This will enable the design team to better judge between the most important elements in the specification.

We will discuss the increasing importance of process design in relation to product design as the design becomes static. Where this occurs is also shown in the design process.

'What', 'how' and 'when' to do product design is important but also included in this book is 'who' should do it. The design circle builds on the proposal of Oakley (1984), suggesting the type of organization and people at different stages of the process. An organic organizational structure is beneficial during most stages of design, but a more mechanistic structure is likely to be more effective in the later stages. Here we confirm the work of others, except that in this book the onset of the mechanistic structure is recommended somewhat later than has previously been proposed.

This design process was developed from research undertaken in industry and was then offered to those managing design in industry. It has been confirmed that it is usable, easy to follow and likely to be effective. The design process, coupled with the knowledge of a product's status, can therefore improve the effectiveness of the management of product design in industry.

2.3 The link with marketing

The work of a marketing department is usually divided into market research (carried out before the design) and marketing (done at the selling end of the design process). Most writers describe marketing at the selling end under the broad headings of the 'four Ps': product, price, promotion and place. This book is ostensibly about the product, but aspects of all parts of marketing are confronted to a greater or lesser extent. We do not contradict other marketing authors, except those (a declining number) that herald the skill of marketeers who can turn a product failure into a success by redirecting it to a different market segment. In our view this is a desperate form of 'fire fighting'. In these cases market research originally identified the wrong market or the wrong product for that market and, as a result, had a design failure. Fortunately, by luck or judgement, these failures were turned into successes, but it must not be forgotten that the majority of designs are failures, and they stay that way (see Section 3.2). We aim to direct the reader towards a design process that relies heavily on good market research that has identified a clear market need and the product idea that will meet these needs. Market research at the end of the design process is effectively being production-led, and therefore against the basic marketing concept of being market-driven. This does not mean that there is not room for 'fine tuning' by the marketing department, at the end of the design process, to comply with the latest information on a changing market to fully meet that market's need.

We do not seriously confront 'promotion', 'price' or 'place', except to give an indication of scale as the product design stabilizes in the market and demand grows. In this book there is also a section on the product life cycle and the 'S'-shaped curve (Section 4.7).

One aspect of marketing worth considering at this stage is why people buy a particular product in preference to another. Some of these reasons are shown in Table 2.1. From the table two points can be made. People buy one product rather than another because they perceive it to have more (or greater) advantages than the competing product (see Part 2, Layer 3). Furthermore, the majority of reasons that make one product apparently more popular or better than another are factors that appear under the broad heading of total design and, therefore, are considered in the following pages. Table 2.1, perhaps more than anything else, demonstrates the importance of product design and the effect that it can have on the saleability of products.

8

Table 2.1 Why people buy products

- ★ Reliability
- ★ Quality
- ★ Safety
- ★ Durability
- ★ Maintainability
- ★ Ease of use (ergonomics)
- Status
- ★ Reputation of company
- ★ Performance (e.g. more economical, faster, more range, quieter, accuracy, etc.)
- ★ Aesthetics/style/fashion
- ★ Finish
- ★ Add-on features/added value
- Availability/speed of delivery/effective distribution
- Credit policy
- ★ Conforming to standards
- ★ User familiarity
- ★ Size
- ★ Packaging
- After-sales service network
- ★ Pollution
- ★ Wider environmental use (temperature, humidity, etc.)
- ★ Shelf life
- ★ Life in service
- ★ Ease of installation
- ★ Comfort
- Legislation (e.g. tax, insurance, etc.)

★ Designed features.

3 The need for good design management

3.1 The importance of effective product design management

Books on how to manage product design first appeared just over 30 years ago and, especially during the past decade there has been a wealth of literature on the subject. This has coincided with the world becoming a far more competitive place. Only 25 years ago there were shortages of many products and waiting lists for consumer durables such as cars and hi-fi equipment. There were too many customers chasing too few products. The situation has now changed: worldwide there is overproduction in cars, ships, steel and many electrical goods. The customer now has plenty of choice for almost every product within a price range.

With this increased choice, consumers have become more aware of the good and bad features of a product, through consumer magazines and advertising, or just by word of mouth. As a result, they select the product that most closely fulfils their opinion of being the best value for money. This is not just price but a wide range of non-price factors such as quality, reliability, aesthetics, delivery, after-sales service, ease of operation, performance, safety and status. Nearly all these price and non-price factors can be related to product design. Therefore good design matters, and good design needs effective managing.

In both the United States and Britain home-based producers have been slow to appreciate the importance of good design. This has resulted in customers selecting an ever-increasing amount of products from countries that do give a higher priority to design. Both countries' share of world markets for manufactured goods has declined steadily, and this has been linked with an increasing demand for imports in their respective home markets. Both have a serious balance of payments problem in manufactured goods and a relative decline in their industrial base, with resulting unemployment and depressed wages in this sector.

Part of the solution is to improve product design to regain competitiveness. Better product design need not cost more (and it can cost less), and if total design is well managed, lost markets may be regained.

In most areas technology is changing faster than ever, and it is generally accepted that a company must continually seek to improve its products if the organization is not to decline and fail. Designing products, though, is expensive at any time, but poorly managed product design can be a very expensive disaster that can cause a company to fail even faster than no design at all. Management must work towards a company-wide approach, integrating marketing, design and production. The message is the same on both sides of the Atlantic: customers have a wide choice in almost every purchase they make, and they are better educated in how to assess value. More are choosing to buy imported products rather than those produced at home. To win back these customers, British and US products must be better by design. Good and efficient design can make the difference between a company surviving or failing, and this can affect the health and economic performance of a nation. The importance of the management of design is therefore being increasingly acknowledged nationally, as shown by the 'Design for Profit Year' in 1986.

However, although the topic of design and its management is currently a 'fashionable' subject for discussion, there has been little hard research in this area. Archer (1986) confirmed this in his report on the International Conference on Engineering Design, held in Hamburg in 1985:

> Far too much of our work in this field, on the evidence of this conference, remains at too high a level of generality. We still make far too many statements that are supported by a very low level of evidence. We have hardly any well founded theory. We do not search diligently enough for evidence that might show where we are wrong.

The US balance of payments deficit may be attributed to the same causes, although, to a great extent, US industry does not suffer from many of the outdated traditions of that of the UK.

The National Science Foundation has a long-term programme 'to establish a scientific foundation of theory, principles and knowledge for engineering design,' and one of its three cornerstones is 'Design Processes'. It is to be hoped that they will learn from work already carried out in this area. There is strong evidence that US industry is conscious of worldwide developments in design process and method, but whether US academia will catch up with changing industrial practices remains problematical, and they may reinforce Archer's (1986) statement.

This book provides the basis for advancing the theory on how to manage design in differing and volatile situations. It should be used by practitioners to improve the overall effectiveness of product design. It does not contain a few simple panaceas that, if followed, ensure success. Successful product design involves hard work and systematic thoroughness throughout the process. Whilst some short cuts are described, following this text and carrying out effective product design is not easy. It is, however, essential when it is realized that the majority of new products are failures. Used correctly it should assist a company to survive in an increasingly competitive world.

3.2 Success and failure of product design

Very broadly, the purpose of this book is to reduce the rate, or chance, of failure in design. There has been much written regarding the failure rates of design and new products and, although there is contradiction in the figures, the general trend shows that the majority of new products are failures. We have taken the failure rates of many products from several researchers and compiled these into the histogram shown in Figure 3.1. Part of the variation in these figures depends on how failure is defined and also over what period of the design, production and marketing cycle the products were investigated. Some started at the initial concept

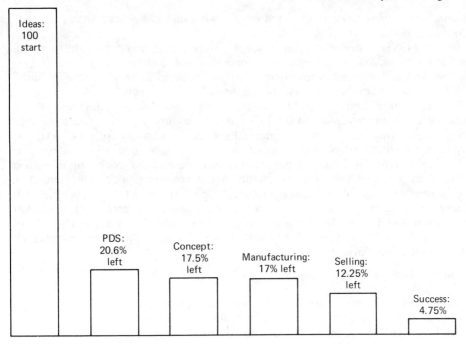

Figure 3.1 Where new product ideas fail. PDS = product design specification

screening, whereas others did not begin to consider the product until it had been brought onto the market.

Failure of a new product has been defined by O'Shaughnessy (1984) as 'occurring whenever management regrets the new product introduction'. Foxall (1984) defines it as 'a product failing to live up to its company expectations in the market'. Conversely, Foxall (1984) defines success as being 'products which met or exceeded their objectives'.

These clearly (and understandably) do not provide a useful measure by which an observer can easily determine a product's failure or success, but researchers into the failure of new product design, almost without exception, have stated that it was unacceptably high and should be reduced if possible.

Although it has been necessary for authors to demonstrate the high rate of failure, the reasons for new product failures are probably of greater interest in any attempt to improve the design of a product and its management.

Cooper (1983) has investigated various case studies by others on the reason for success and failure of new products. He has ascertained that new products are more likely to be successful if the company understands user requirements and provides 'market-pull' type products. It is also an advantage to have a product champion and effective communications both inside and outside the organization. The most common reason for product failure was found to be overwhelmingly due to inadequate market analysis, and this had not altered over 17 years of research. Conversely, for product success 'correct identification of an existing demand was the critical common ingredient'. This was a typical main finding along with efficient development, key individuals and a clear product advantage over the competition, although there were 'no easy explanations for what makes a new product a success' (Cooper, 1983).

Turner (1983) states that: 'Surveys have shown that about two thirds of all products considered to be technical successes are commercial failures.' This suggests that failure lies in the original market research, in 'concept vulnerability' (Pugh, 1984a), or in the way that the final product is marketed.

The differences between technical success and commercial failure emphasize those between engineering and total design. For technical success you need top-grade engineering design; for commercial success highest-quality total design is required, which incorporates the former; neither is a substitute for the other.

Corfield (1979) has identified the separation of design and marketing in British industry as a major contributory factor to the country's poor achievement in commercially successful innovative product design, and Twiss (1980) has observed: 'There is substantial evidence from both sides of the Atlantic that a market orientation is still woefully absent in many decisions and that is a major source of failure.' Bright (1968) has listed the causes of success and failure from his research into technical innovation:

The most critical of these are:
(1) Market orientation
(2) Relevance to the organization's corporate objectives
(3) An effective project selection and evaluation system
(4) Effective project management and control
(5) A source of creative ideas
(6) An organization receptive to innovation
(7) Commitment by one of a few individuals.

Such findings have been of use in guiding us towards important areas of investigation and provide a framework on which to structure this prescriptive design process manual.

Looking again at Figure 3.1 we can see that relatively few products fail after the product design specification has been compiled. This is not surprising, for after the specification has been written it is possible, with most products, to identify a concept. It is usually also possible to detail and manufacture it, although several potential new products fail at that stage. Therefore, over half of the products that reach the specification stage are put onto the market and, of these, nearly two-thirds fail.

Clearly, the aim must be to ensure, as far as possible, that the great majority of new products that reach the selling stage are going to be a success. This means identifying much earlier those products that are likely to fail and then abandoning them before a significant investment has been made.

The next section describes where design managers should direct their emphasis for greatest design efficiency.

3.3 The low-cost end of design

Some researchers have compiled tables showing the costs of various stages of design. Their results have been used in Table 3.1 where these costs have been shown next to the main steps on the design activity model (Figure 3.2) for ease of comparison. This figure demonstrates that the cost of the early stages of the process

Table 3.1 The percentage costs of new product design

Terms used	Mansfield et al. (1971)	US Dept. Commerce (Mansfield, 1968)	Viewing (1980)	Bass (1969)	Buggie (1981)	Buggie (1981)	Booz Allen and Hamilton (1968)		
							Success	Failures	Total
Applied research	9.5	5–10							
Business analysis	7.6								
Specification			10–15	22	83	30	2	14	16
Concept									
Verification									
Development			10–25						
Detail design							12	45	57
Testing/prototype or pilot	29.1	10–20	20–30			13	4	6	10
Plant				58					
Tooling and manufacturing facilities	36.9	40–60	30–60						
Manufacturing	9.1	5–15							
Start-up						67			
Marketing start-up	7.7	10–25		11	17				
Selling							12	5	17
Commercialization									

14

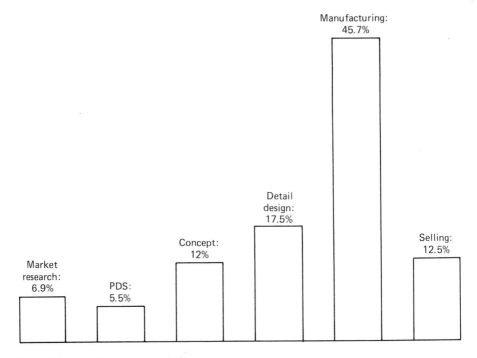

Figure 3.2 Cost of new product design

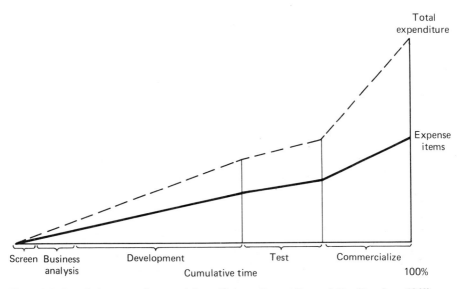

Figure 3.3 Cumulative expenditure and time. (Source: Booz Allen and Hamilton Inc., 1968)

of product design, where the main design direction is taken, is at the low-cost end, and costs are much greater in the later stages.

As can be seen in Figure 3.3, the cost of designing a product rises geometrically as it approaches production. An error made at the low-cost end of design can often get carried into the high-cost end or into production. The design process, as described, concentrates the work at the early, low-cost end of design, helping to ensure that problems or errors in the proposed product are confronted and eliminated at this stage, thus avoiding expensive correction or product abandonment later.

Johne (1985) refers to work at the front end of design as being relatively low cost:

> We regard the increased emphasis given to 'up front analysis' in many firms as a particularly important refinement of product innovation initiation procedures...one R&D manager expressed it as follows. At the concept stage it's worth spending up to $100000 on this – sometimes more. The down-side risk to the company is far less than letting the market test a fully developed new product costing, say, $5 million (p. 162).

Therefore it can be argued that if the problems and possible sources of error could be confronted at the early stages of design there would be a greater possibility that errors in the product – in market research, design or production – could be eliminated at this stage and that these errors, or even wrong products, would be prevented from being carried through into the high-cost end of design (i.e. production).

Furthermore, if an effective process of product screening was developed a large number of product ideas could be considered: most would be eliminated at this low-cost end of design and those that were not eliminated would have a greater chance of success. It is unimportant that a large number of ideas are screened before a successful product is found and that the failure rate of new product ideas will continue to be high. In fact, it may increase, but the failure rate of designs actually developed into a product and successfully put onto the market will decrease. 'Weeding out' of potential design failures before the stage when high development costs are incurred will reduce the overall cost of new product design, even though a larger number of new product ideas have been considered.

With this in mind, we believed that a method for eliminating the 'wrong product', and ensuring that only products with potentially a greater chance of success should be designed, was an essential part of product design and its management. The front end, being also the low-cost end of design, could be expanded without a significant increase in the overall design project cost or time. This would lead to a more 'efficient' design process, that is, retaining product quality but reducing overall design cost and time. Therefore, from the literature on product failures, on where these failures occur and on the cost of various stages of design we can deduce that the overall emphasis in design management should be at the front end.

The ideal situation is shown in Figure 3.4. In this the front-end work is expanded so that many more product ideas can be considered. Most of these will be rejected with almost no investment in them, but with a larger number of product ideas, those that remain will be potentially of higher quality – they are more likely to be a market success.

Having introduced a system that weeds out potential product failures at an earlier stage, the subsequent stages of the total design process can proceed but with few products being abandoned. The majority of designs that proceed beyond the

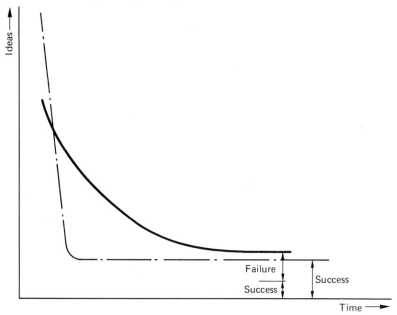

Figure 3.4 New product elimination. —— Current situation. ––– An ideal situation?

early stages of the process will be put on the market and the success rate of these will be high. Of course, the situation shown in Figure 3.4 is the ideal case and is unlikely to be achieved in practice. However, this should be your aim, and it has been ours in compiling the design process described in Part 2 of this book. Remember that the front-end of design is low cost when compared to the subsequent stages, so what is described is the low-cost option – better and cheaper design.

One of the fundamental parts of this design process is the principle of 'product status', which is described in the next chapter.

4 Successful design through product status

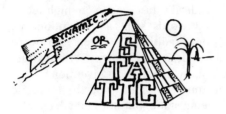

4.1 What is product status?

This design system uses the concept of product status to direct the design manager. The concept of product design as being different at two boundaries was hypothesized in the work of Pugh and Smith (1976). In Pugh (1983) the two boundaries are called static and dynamic, maximum innovation and synthesis occurring at the dynamic boundary and minimum synthesis at the conventional static boundary (Figure 4.1).

On a macro level, quite independently, Klein (1977) has used the same terms to describe a similar process shown using S-shaped curves of 'performance function' against a base of time. He describes dynamic behaviour as that 'associated with pioneering new products and processes' (p.4). He later continues: 'The key

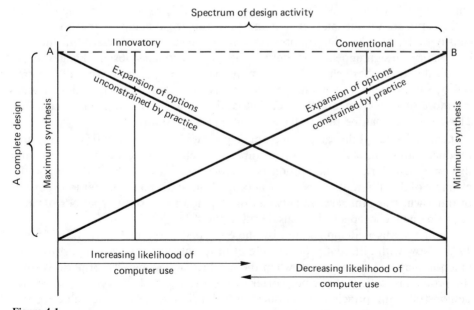

Figure 4.1

difference between static and dynamic processes is that whereas the former involves types of change that can be predicted on the basis of initial conditions the latter involves quite unpredictable changes in initial conditions' (p.12).

Several others have observed a similar process of some products being dynamic designs, but using words such as 'innovative', 'radical', 'fast' and even 'high-tech', and other products being static designs using words such as 'evolutionary', 'incremental', 'dominant', 'mature', 'slow' or 'traditional'. Often the word 'innovation' is used (wrongly) to describe static design as shown in the extract below from Johne (1985). Innovation, by definition, requires an invention.

Some writers have observed that at certain times (without using these precise words) products are dynamic and progress to being static, but not many have also observed that a static product can become dynamic again.

Kuhn (1962) states that scientists in any field and at any time possess a set of shared belief's about the world and for that time the set constitutes the dominant paradigm. The results are small steps towards progress. After the paradigm shift progress is fast, though fraught with tension. New discoveries are made to support the new belief system and scientific revolution occurs. This phenomenon of science is also found in design. Johne (1985) states:

> Broadly speaking there are two types [of product innovation]: 1) Radical product innovation and 2) incremental product innovation. Radical product innovation involves using advances in technology to offer customers a new line of products. Incremental product innovation involves using existing technology to extend an established product line or improve product performance to a certain degree (p.11).

Therefore over a period of time changes occur in a product design, gradually improving what Klein (1977) calls its 'performance function'. Occasionally a new design appears on the market and the performance function is improved quite considerably, but then these improvements again become gradual until the next new radical design appears. Therefore with some products design changes are of a radical nature where changes occur in the basic concept: these types of products can be said to have a 'dynamic product status'. In other products design changes are more of an incremental nature, that is, the basic concept remains unchanged. These products can be said to have a 'static product status'.

It can be deduced that at any one time a product has either a static or a dynamic product status, but over a period of time products move between the static and dynamic boundaries. Some products (as described by Pugh, 1983, using the example of the differential gear) stay at or near the static boundary for long periods of time, whereas others move between the boundaries in shorter periods of time, requiring new concepts to be considered in their design.

Product status is demonstrated by the S-shaped curve in Figure 4.2 (Hollins, 1988). Now with different products and at different times the rise in performance function may be greater or less when the product is dynamic (b), or periods when the product is static (a) may be shorter or longer. The S-shaped curve, therefore, demonstrates the principle of product status but in itself is of little value for two reasons. First, it may be possible to put some value on the performance function,

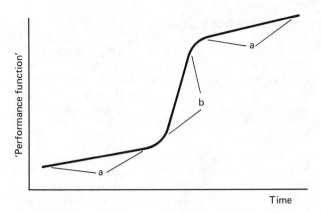

Figure 4.2

as has been attempted by Klein (1977) and others, but even this is of dubious value. For example, how can the aesthetics of, say, a watch be measured or graded next to its weight? Secondly, even if the performance function could be measured the timebase could only be provided in hindsight.

On the other hand, if it was possible to demonstrate that a particular product at a particular time was either static or dynamic, then product status starts to become useful. If it could be further demonstrated that a product's status was static, dynamic or changing either now or in the near future then product status takes on a new value.

In its basic form if a product can be identified as being static then only incremental changes would be needed, whereas if it was dynamic then it would be known that new concepts need to be considered. This would be valuable in itself to a product design team, but the principle can be taken much further. In the paper by Pugh and Smith (1976) it has been shown that computer-aided design is more likely to be applicable for designing a product demanding 'minimum synthesis'. Therefore if a particular product's status could be identified as dynamic the company's management would know that investment in computer-aided design for this product would probably not be worthwhile, as conventional draughting is likely to be more adaptable and more effective. This reasoning could be taken further with many other design activities or 'disciplines' that are used in product design, production and marketing. If these could be broadly divided into activities that are more suited for products which are dynamic, those that are more suited for products which are newly static or static for a long time, and those that are necessary irrespective of the product status, the design manager would know which disciplines should be emphasized and which could be diminished when designing that particular product.

The key to the whole process, therefore, is in being able to identify a product's status, that is, factors that would keep a product static or dynamic or, perhaps most important, show when the status was likely to change, and then stipulating which design disciplines should accompany a particular product status and when they should be used.

4.2 The need to look for product status

As described in the previous section, the method for improving the success of product design lies in the principle of product status. This will involve a company giving its products the correct status and being organized for maximum efficiency with regard to this status. It must also be able to detect signs of changing product status, so that it can react quickly and not be overtaken by the competition. Carpenter *et al.* (1986) have discussed a similar effect in what they call the 'innovation cycle':

> Business firms need a relatively stable technology in order to cut costs ... However, in today's fast moving world, stable technologies are harder and harder to come by ... Any technology can be improved for a time, but eventually a point will be reached where any further improvements will require prohibitively expensive inputs with no significant improvement. To remain competitive, this is exactly where firms have to seek technological innovation.

Carpenter *et al.* suggest that static plateaus are becoming shorter: this may be true, but is not so with every product. However, by being unaware of a product's status they imply that innovation should be sought only when incremental or static design is exhausted. We suggest that, to remain competitive, innovation is usually required, and can be detected as being necessary earlier than this point, when the product is dynamic again. The examples given by Carpenter *et al.* (cash registers, typewriters, word processors) could all have been detected as being dynamic much earlier than the actual decline of the manufacturers of the replaced technology and before static improvements were exhausted. But were the companies looking for this change and did they have the tools? We suspect not.

At least Carpenter *et al.* realize that products do alter from being static to dynamic. Many companies get locked into only undertaking static design, as Abernathy and Wayne (1974) state: 'Industry can easily become the prisoner of its own massive investment in low cost production and the organizational systems that support it.'

This was also observed by Skinner (1986), who found that although US manufacturers have made 'near heroic efforts' to improve productivity, many are still losing market share. He points to this effort being misdirected by improving workers' efficiency without making improvements in 'strategic resources' such as 'quality, reliability, delivery, short lead times, customer service, rapid product introduction, flexible capacity and efficient capital deployment'. It could be argued that although these strategic resources are important, the failure of some of these companies may be that they are aiming to produce more efficiently a product that the market does not altogether want. The product may be dynamic and further innovation or a new concept may be required. Skinner recommends what will be shown later in this book to be only static design disciplines. However, he does state that 'Managers under relentless pressure to maximize productivity resist innovation'.

It is understandable why companies do not want to regard their products as dynamic again even though it may be in their best interests, as Dowdy and Nikolchev (1986) observed:

> Established companies often are comfortable with traditional industry structures and have invested significant resources in labour, product and process technologies, management and financial systems, and marketing channels based on commonly accepted precepts of competitive advantage.

Companies need to determine and act on their products' status, even though it may be an uncomfortable and disruptive process. This is the only way in which they can ensure their survival.

However, looking for product status will not result in continuous concept change: there are static plateaus. Products must be manufactured on a static plateau, even if they are dynamic, in order to achieve production stability. Since continuous innovation also means continuous change this would probably not be acceptable to customers if they have bought equipment to interface with the older technology (e.g. videotapes). Products improve in steps. An example of this, relating to aircraft design improvements, was identified by Miller and Sawyers (1968): 'The picture of the aircraft industry where the commercial part of its development is concerned, is thus not one of steady technical progress but of widely spaced jumps' (p.1). This can be explained by Klein (1977), who states:

> Changing affiliation is not always costless. For example when airline companies buy a new type of airliner, mechanics must be retrained and a significant investment in spare parts is required. However, as costs are reduced more and more, at some point we should expect to observe a marked change in affiliation. According to people employed in development and production of new airliners it is hardly worthwhile to develop a new airliner which will only result in a 5 per cent cost saving. But a 20 per cent cost saving is a quite different matter.

This suggests that those developing new aircraft do appreciate one aspect of product status and have identified the 'extent' of the innovation, in terms of improved performance, required to end the static plateau and make the product dynamic again. They have shown the need to look for product status in their design.

We shall describe other areas which manufacturers should also research in order to identify their products' status and thereby direct their best course of action. With the benefit of hindsight, it can be shown that with certain products, prior knowledge of product status and its use may have directed companies towards a more successful course of action. Five product types are taken as examples:

1. Clockwork/electronic watches;
2. The Sinclair C5 electric car;
3. Videorecording machines;
4. Cars;
5. Slide rules calculators.

4.2.1 Clockwork/electronic watches

When the LCD display and microchip technology made the electronic watch possible in 1970 it became apparent that a more accurate but potentially cheaper watch had been feasible two years before it appeared on the market. At that time Swiss watchmakers were larger and richer than any of the new companies and they could have bought into the technology. However, they did nothing, and as a result their market seriously declined and is only recently increasing again. They could have appreciated that the potential advantages of the new electronic watch were about to end the static plateau.

Now that watch design is static again, the fortunes of some companies have subsequently been improved by their recognition of two aspects of static design – aesthetics and fashion. The Swiss company SMH has used these concepts in their 'Swatch' to build a new market. The basic, reliable and inexpensive product is kept 'fresh' by an ever-changing appearance.

4.2.2 The Sinclair C5 electric car

It should have been obvious to Sinclair that the design of the C5 would not end the static plateau and could not do so until a significant breakthrough in battery technology had been made which would allow them to build a vehicle of comparative performance to a car or until the cost of oil had reached prohibitive heights. Neither had occurred, and therefore the C5 was almost certain not to cause the product to become dynamic again. Thus it was destined to fail as a replacement for the car. It may have been more successful if it had been aimed at a different market (see Part 3, Chapter 8).

4.2.3 Videorecording machines

The originators of videorecording machines failed to appreciate that the technology had reached a point where a cost-effective consumer product could be marketed. In effect, the dynamic phase of the design had come to an end, and a suitable 'injection' of the disciplines of static design (i.e. process design for low-cost manufacture) would produce a machine at a price within the range of a wide market – a static plateau. The originators all failed to take this step and all declined and the Japanese companies who concentrated on this aspect of the design, using the originators' innovations, took over the market.

4.2.4 Cars

Although basic car design has been static for some years, from 1966 onwards car companies concentrated more of their effort and resources on the way in which a car is manufactured rather than on its actual design. Once again the Japanese led the way, producing cars effectively and at a lower cost than that of their competitors, thereby taking a lead in world markets. Ten years later the European manufacturers also started to adopt this policy. Having (basically) static design, they maximized on the static design disciplines to produce more efficiently. It could have been possible to predict this emphasis earlier and to match the Japanese in process design.

4.2.5 Slide rules/calculators

The first electronic calculator was made by the Bell Punch Company of London in 1963. Therefore the advent of the calculator was known some ten years before it was produced as a low-cost replacement for the slide rule. Slide rule manufacturers were never rich or skilled enough to obtain entry into this market. However, knowing that the product was dynamic again they could have foreseen their eventual demise and diversified – they did nothing, and declined.

It can be seen that the simple expedient of knowing and using product status can have a fundamental effect on the health and sometimes the survival of your company. From the product examples given above, in many cases the threat to the end of the static plateau comes from a company not currently in the same industry, as has been noted by Klein (1977).

The above examples suggest that the ability to innovate is of fundamental importance to a company. Drucker (1974) has written that 'An established company which, in an age demanding innovation, is not capable of innovation is doomed to decline and extinction'.

Certainly there is sufficient evidence to show that technology is changing faster than ever (Carpenter *et al.*, 1986; Ansoff, 1982; Nyström, 1979), and company management must be aware that innovation may become necessary to keep its products competitive. However, it has been estimated (Ingersoll, 1985) that about 70 per cent of Britain's engineering output comes from 'traditional' engineering industries who have well-established products and where incremental design improvements may be more effective than innovation. Having a traditional, well-established product, though, does not mean that a company can ignore innovation all the time. If a competitor or competitors find a way of ending the static plateau, thus making the product dynamic again, the established companies will then have to engage in 'reactive' design to timescales and conditions not of their choosing. By appreciating product status it becomes possible to show when a product design is static and innovation need not be considered for that product, or, alternatively, it is dynamic and innovation and change is required.

4.3 The advantage of knowing the product status

You will discover that product status can be a powerful means of directing design management towards areas which are of greater importance in product design. There are also several advantages for a company to know its product status, and these are described below. Some of these are dealt with more fully elsewhere in this book, but it is useful to list them together:

1. Knowing the product status indicates whether changes need (or are likely) to be innovative or incremental.
2. Knowing if changes need (or are likely) to be innovative or incremental allows a company to direct its emphases in design, production and aspects of marketing through the design plan.
3. Knowing the product status makes certain elements of the product design specification more important and others less so; e.g. status dynamic, standards less important, patents more important.
4. Knowing the product status can simplify the design process; e.g. seeking new concepts in the design model will be of less (and sometimes of no) importance with a truly static design.
5. A static product which becomes dynamic again can indicate when design and research should cease on the old concept. For example, major developments in thermionic valves were made by the Mullard Company some years after the invention of the transistor. Design effort could have been redirected to an area with a greater long-term potential. 'When faced with a technological threat, dominant firms frequently have responded with even greater reliance on obsolete technology (e.g. telegraph/telephone; vacuum tube/transistor; core memory/semi-conductor memory)' (Tushman and Nadler, 1986). As another example, the latest developments in digital recording tapes suggest a greatly reduced product life cycle for compact discs.
6. If a product is known to be static it is possible to identify the extent of an innovation necessary to end the static plateau. This can direct a company to:
   (a) Not develop a new technology (e.g. electric cars until a low-cost, low-weight, high-power battery is discovered);
   (b) Develop the new technology (e.g. anti-lock braking systems for cars).

7. If a company does not have sufficient disciplines associated with the product status of the new design it can aid its decision on whether:
   (a) It should not attempt to enter a market (e.g. a batch production company should not enter the match industry): 'Late entry to markets is only possible by large companies' (Rothwell, 1985).
   (b) It should consider leaving a particular product market.
8. Knowing the product status can show if investment should be directed by the company towards process or product design (e.g. telescopic handler manufacturers should direct investment towards process design).
9. Knowing the product status can show if investment should be directed by an outside funding source (e.g. NRDC) into the research direction being considered by a company or academic institution.
10. As a large company (relative to the competition) benefits from a design being static and a small one may benefit from a design being dynamic (smaller companies tend to react faster to change), a large company should aim for static products and a small one should aim for dynamic products.
11. If a product design is static and looks like remaining static for some time, market share becomes increasingly important, as this enables greater volumes in relation to the competition and therefore a greater degree of static design to be included. This will allow the company to benefit from economies of scale and lower cost production to further enhance its competitive edge. Therefore if a product appears to be static for some time in the future a company should aim to increase its market share. Larger market share leads to economies of scale, improved learning curves, larger (bulk) purchases of materials, better machine usage and more sales outlets.
12. Knowing that a competitive company is operating with a particular status can indicate if its new products are likely to be static or dynamic, and can aid planning of its defence against competition.
13. If a product is known to be static the future is more predictable. Therefore corporate planning is easier and can be undertaken with a greater confidence in its accuracy and the product design specification is easier to write.

Having described the advantages of knowing the status of products, in the next section we will show the factors that make a product static or dynamic.

4.4 Factors that make a product static or dynamic

The following have all been determined through our research in industry.

Factors that make a product static
1. Limited design time
2. Customers not willing to change
3. Stable effective product design specification
4. Dedicated machinery, automation, CAD, purchasing new machinery
5. Few large producers
6. A decreasing or stable number of producers
7. More process design than product design
8. Poor market research
9. Stable technology (product static for a long time)
10. Market infrastructure based on existing design

11. Stable/improving environment for existing design (commodities and resources)
12. Conformance standards
13. User familiarity (performance standards)
14. Restricted design (at any level, e.g. value analysis, CAD)
15. Using experience in design
16. Using imitation in design
17. Restricted product design specification (e.g. same sales outlet, extension of existing range)
18. Using rationalization or commonality of parts between several product components in design
19. Assembling components made by others
20. Product interfaces with, or is part of, an assembly made elsewhere
21. Product available in its present form for a long time (static)
22. Insufficient design/finance resources/management commitment

Factors that make a product dynamic
 1. Adequate time allowed for design
 2. Customers willing to change
 3. Change in product design specification
 4. Flexible machinery, subcontracted manufacture
 5. Many small producers
 6. An increasing number of producers
 7. More emphasis on product design than process design
 8. Wide effective market research (innovation seeking, market pull)
 9. Technology advancement
10. No market infrastructure (or infrastructure also suitable for new design)
11. Changing environment (legislation, economic climate, resources)
12. No conformance standards
13. Open management design guidelines
14. Companies seeking new concepts

We have identified various factors that can cause a product to retain its existing status or can act to change it. These factors can work on two levels: those that operate within an organization (microfactors) and those outside the organization's control which affect the environment in which the product is being sold (macrofactors). A company may be able to change the factors within its makeup to match the product status of the market environment, but, of course, it is far more difficult to change the environment of the market in which a product is being sold. A company's product status should be 'in step' with that of its environment. It can be seen that there is a certain amount of overlap between the various factors but the following broad categories can be identified. Initially those factors in the environment that affect the product's status are described.

4.4.1 Macrofactors

1. Infrastructure
If this is large and based on the existing design concept there is less chance of a new design replacing it. With the internal combustion engine, for example, there is a large infrastructure which acts to prevent or restrict change. This includes fuel supply, servicing, spares, sales outlets and manufacturing facilities. There is much

experience associated with the car engine in its current form, and a radical change would require a large amount of retraining so that all operatives associated with its manufacture could become familiar with a new design. Such a design may have a greater chance of success if it can utilize much of the existing infrastructure, which suggests that if a large infrastructure is already in place for a particular product, any new design should not be too radical.

2. The same or no infrastructure based on the existing design
If an existing static product can be easily replaced without the need to alter any peripheral organization it is potentially more able to become dynamic again. For example, the preference for tumble driers instead of spin driers or transistor radios instead of valve radios is partly due to the later design using the same selling and servicing infrastructures, which were no more difficult to instal than those replaced.

3. Performance standards (user familiarity)
With most products there is an interface with other products, and a change in the design of one can mean that those other products must also be changed. This will usually result in an inconvenience to (and loss of familiarity by) potential customers which they may not be prepared to accept, with a subsequent extension of the static plateau. There are many examples where an improved design was accepted because it did not interface with a popular standard. For example, the design for music cassettes has remained virtually unaltered since it became widely available in 1968. The VHS system for videorecording machines was technically not as advanced as the Philips 2000 system, but one of the reasons the latter failed in the market was that their tapes were incompatible with the VHS system. The new 9 mm Sony videotape can be supplied with a dummy cartridge case to fit the existing, now standard, VHS design. A familiar, well-entrenched design can be quite difficult to replace in the market and is therefore another factor that keeps a product static.

4. Conformance standards
Standards laid down for products and often enforced by law can restrict a designer's freedom and can be both an indication of a static product and a reason for the design to remain static. Conformance standards such as those set by BSI, VDI, Underwriters, etc. take some years to be compiled, and therefore are often an indication that the product design is static; standards tend not to be written for a product that is in a continual state of change. Furthermore, as it is often a requirement to conform to these standards the design cannot change except in a peripheral or aesthetic way. Such an example is the UK three-pin plug, which is oversized, overengineered, heavy, and ugly, but new designs are unlikely to be dynamic as long as they must comply with BS 1363.

5. No conformance standards
If there are no standards to which a product must conform there is more freedom for the design team to discard the existing concept and introduce a dynamic design. Most vehicles are limited in their design by having to conform to various standards such as brakes, lights, types of tyres, etc. It is generally easy to see designs that have to be limited by standards which determine shape and material use. Art objects are generally free of standards, which allows greater flexibility in design and the ability to use a new concept. A lack of a standard may be an indication in itself that the product may be dynamic.

6. A product being available in its present form for a long time

The existence of a product on the market for a long time appears to generate a 'momentum' that further extends its potential design life. This is probably an effect of the combination of other factors described in this section. It has been shown that it is in the interests of companies with dedicated machinery to keep the product static. The longer a product is static, the more likely it is that the producers will have dedicated machinery resulting in limits to change. Conformance standards may have been written and customers become familiar with the existing product or need it to interface with it: for example, a replacement shock absorber should fit the existing mountings available for it. A whole infrastructure becomes built around an existing design the longer it is available, and some of that may be quite minor in nature (e.g. the 2CV Owners Club), but these will exert pressure against change. The net effect is that the longer a product design has been static, the more likely it is to remain static.

7. A decreasing or stable number of manufacturers

When a product becomes static process design becomes increasingly more important. The resulting more efficient manufacture reduces costs, and the larger companies, who are more likely to benefit from economies of scale, are most able to do this. As the product becomes static the larger companies benefit and the smaller companies either decline or are taken over by larger ones (unless they can find a safe market niche). Therefore a declining number of manufacturers which are increasing in size is an indication of a static product. This is apparent in the car industry, where over the years most smaller companies have been merged with larger ones, resulting in a few very powerful conglomerates producing a basically static design with an emphasis on low-cost production. Microcomputer manufacturers originally tended to be small, but over the past few years as the product has been on the static plateau the number of firms has quickly declined and mergers have made these companies larger. The mainframe industry reached this point some 15 years earlier.

8. An increasing number of (small) producers

This is the converse of the above paragraph. Small manufacturers have a history of producing more technological breakthroughs than large ones, one reason being that they have less to gain from a product design being static. They can also adapt and change faster than larger companies and also it is easier to arrange an organic structure in a small company, which has been shown to be more conducive to innovation. An increasing number of small manufacturers of a particular product is therefore an indication that a product design is dynamic or potentially dynamic.

9. Customers not willing to change

A dynamic design may be produced but it will not end the static plateau unless customers are prepared to accept it in preference to an existing design. This may be due to some of the reasons already mentioned, as well as perceived value for money, usefulness, ease of use or even some unquantifiable reason such as style or image, etc. An obvious example is battery-powered vehicles for personal transport, which customers have not been prepared to accept due to their low speed and limited range. The mere existence of a new design is not sufficient to make a product dynamic. It must be a design that customers want, and therefore must be demonstrably better than the product it is intended to replace.

10. Customers willing to change

The converse of the above paragraph is also true. A new product that can be demonstrated to have advantages over one already in the market will encourage customers to adopt the new product. Again this may only be a perceived advantage which can be nurtured through product presentation and advertising. Customers are encouraged by products that appear to improve their quality of life, are labour saving or have a better image. Generally, though, an improved performance at an acceptable price is the most effective means by which a new dynamic design will be accepted to end the existing static plateau. An example could be the complete replacement of monochrome by colour televisions when the prices of the latter are lowered to an 'acceptable' level.

11. Technical advance

This is the main factor that can make a design become dynamic again. It can be technical advances inside or outside the company or an industry. Many examples are available (e.g. from piston engines to jet engines in the aircraft industry, or from cyclohexane to curare derivatives in the field of anaesthetics). The rate of technical advance in many areas of industry is accelerating, and therefore in these industries product design will more often be dynamic.

12. Stable technology

With a stable technology there is less likelihood of a product becoming dynamic. A company needs to believe that the technology associated with a particular product is stable, even only temporarily, or that changes can be built into the existing product (sub-innovations) to make the investment commitments which lead to the other static factors mentioned elsewhere in this section. A stable technology is an aid to production stability which makes production investments more easily justified.

13. Government action/legislation

This is often overlooked by designers, but government action and legislation can have a considerable effect on the likely success of new designs. A government may create or reduce the competitiveness or desirability of certain products through, for example, taxation, safety legislation or legal acceptability. This can also create a potential new market for a dynamic design that avoids these problems or which can service new markets.

The Health and Safety at Work etc. Act (1974) and BS 5740 ('Safeguarding Machinery') spurred a whole new industry of safety products, many of which involved entirely new concepts using technology, such as infrared light guards and optical fibre guards replacing the slower mechanical methods. Similarly, legislation on restricting lorry drivers' hours created the market for and design of tachographs. Conversely, the limited amount of design work on diesel engines for cars undertaken in Britain and the USA compared to that in Europe has been blamed on the British rates of taxation on fuel which results in only a small differential between the cost of petrol and Derv. On the Continent this differential is much greater, creating a larger market for diesel-engined cars and greater design emphasis in this direction. Taxation has also had an effect on cigarette smoking, and has created a market for smoking cures or substitutes.

14. Commodities and resources

Relative changes between the cost and availability of certain commodities and some resources and even the general economic climate can make a product design become dynamic. Higher disposable income can cause the design of new products where none existed before, such as tumble driers, microwave ovens and compact disc players. Such products are generally not widely available in the Third World, where disposable incomes are less. Another example is the effect that the quadrupling of the price of oil in 1974 had on the market for oil-fired central heating. This was greatly reduced, but dynamic designs in both gas and electrical central heating boilers were encouraged.

15. Stable or improving environment for the existing design

If a product design is static, and acceptable to a particular market, and if there are no changes in that market environment, there is less pressure to alter the design. An improving environment may even enhance the attraction of the existing design and extend its design life. The recent falls in the price of oil have given oil-fired power stations a new lease of life, which has resulted in lower investment in new, 'alternative' power generation (e.g. wind and wave) and has caused coal-fired stations to be less viable with a subsequent reduction in the price of coal. This also makes other forms of transport less attractive compared with oil/petrol-driven vehicles.

16. Changing environment

The reverse of the above is also a factor that can make a product dynamic. Legislation has already been mentioned, but a changing economic climate or variations in the cost of commodities and resources will encourage dynamic design in certain areas.

4.4.2 Microfactors

We have identified the following factors that make a product static or dynamic which are within a company and therefore a company may often have control over them. There is a difference between products being truly static and those being treated as static when they may be potentially dynamic.

1. Stable effective product design specifications

If a product's design specification is the best that is available within a current technology the product design is unlikely to change. This specification may originate from one company but may also develop and grow from various companies over a period of time. The design of familiar products often demonstrates those that have an effective product design specification which can extend a static plateau almost indefinitely (e.g. paperclips, safety pins and staples).

2. A change in the product design specification

A significant change in the product design specification brought about by new or changing customer demand, possibly identified by market research, may end the static plateau of a product. For example, in heavy-duty shock absorbers used on tanks the UK Ministry of Defence, after computer simulation of ideal suspension performance, changed the damper requirements to beyond those possible with the technology then available. These necessitated a new concept and a new dynamic design, resulting in significantly improved damper characteristics. Similarly, the requirement for a rough terrain forklift truck to have a forward reach identified by market research resulted in a product design specification which indicated a vehicle significantly different from the existing forklift truck. The new dynamic design was the telescopic handler, for which demand now greatly exceeds the RTFL in the agricultural market.

3. Restricted product design specification

With several companies it has been noted that the opportunity for a product to become dynamic again has been limited by restrictions imposed in the product design specification. For example, one company used a chart on which were specific requests for data that limited the design to a variation of an existing concept, thus ensuring that in this company the basic concept would remain unchanged. Another would make any kind of shock absorber as long as it was a telescopic one. This company was foregoing some exciting, and more acceptable, innovations that would have increased its market and its chances of survival. It is therefore important to ensure that one's company, or design team, is not unnecessarily, or inadvertently, restricting its product design specification and missing new product opportunities.

4. Using imitation in design

If all the manufacturers of a particular product are copying each other it is unlikely that a design will progress from being static. Imitation of each other by companies in a particular industry may explain why most dynamic designs tend to originate from companies not previously operating in that market. Again the car industry is a good example of this. Each manufacturer tends to copy the others, keeping the design basically static. Of course, it only requires one of the larger manufacturers to adopt a successful dynamic design for others to attempt to copy it.

5. Companies seeking new concepts

Unless a company makes a conscious effort to seek a new concept the design will remain static, but once a company starts to do so it is likely that a new dynamic design will result, although companies actively seeking new concepts are more unusual than most people would expect. Most companies appear to be content with incremental changes to an existing concept.

6. Using experience in design

When designing a product it is common to use existing or extensions to practices that have been tried and are known to work. This can be a good thing, as familiarity with aspects of a design can make the overall product more reliable, easier and faster to design, and often cheaper. However, this can also make new designs very similar to existing ones and keep the product static. Klein (1977) has shown that reliance on experience is one of the reasons technical change often occurs away from the existing manufacturers of the product.

7. Products made by assembling components made by others

When a company is making a product from a series of components made by others it has less freedom to produce a dynamic design. For example, industrial vehicle producers often base their design on bought-in components such as engines, standard electrical parts, wheels, tyres, and, in some cases, tractor skids. These determine most of the characteristics of their vehicles.

The converse can be argued in that it is easier to 'switch off' an outside supplier to allow a dynamic design, as demonstrated by companies such as Casio, who rely entirely on subcontractors for their production, allowing them to make radical design changes easily and quickly. This reverse effect, though, is not so clearly (or so often) demonstrated in product design in the UK, Europe or the USA, except in the fast-moving consumer goods industry.

8. Purchasing new (dedicated) machinery

If a company has invested in machinery which can only be used to produce existing or similar products it will not be in the interests of the company to design a product that cannot use this dedicated machinery unless it is approaching the end of its useful life and unless the dynamic design has a significant advantage over the existing static design. This includes CAD, which is less effective when dealing with new concepts. In process industries, where large amounts of capital are invested in existing production plant, any product changes are made with reluctance, and only when it can be demonstrated that such changes can be made profitably. The result is a tendency to keep the existing static product, with perhaps only minor changes.

9. Flexible machinery

A production process that is kept flexible is more able to cope with new designs, especially dynamic ones. Small companies tend to have more flexible machinery that can be used on a variety of products, subcontract jobbing shops and tool makers being an obvious example. As an extreme case, there is a cocktail-stick manufacturer who must change the range of his novelty sticks monthly to keep in fashion. Any dedicated tooling bought for this market must be written off inside one month and is not purchased unless unavoidable. A company with flexible machinery is therefore more predisposed to make a product become or remain dynamic than one with dedicated machinery.

The effect of new technology, including robots, confuses the picture. It is debatable how flexible a robot is regarding production quantities versus programming time and also in the flexibility of the actual robot. A welding robot can only weld, and therefore products may need to be welded rather than assembled with adhesives. In theory, robots should be used as flexible tools, but in practice the justification of their cost generally means that large production quantities are needed. Therefore they tend to be used as dedicated machinery (e.g. in car plants and for the manufacture of 'white goods').

10. Automation

The effects of automation are similar to those of dedicated machinery or CAD but its use actually keeps a product static by maintaining existing production levels with dedicated machinery or restricting new concepts in CAD. Automation may, in theory, allow dynamic design, but in practice this tends not to occur. It can take many forms, and claims are made by its manufacturers of adaptability or flexibility which allows variation in a product and for 'one-offs' to become viable. Two factors, though, contradict those claims and make automation a factor that is likely to keep a product static. Initially the cost of automation is relatively high, and prior to an investment decision being made this expense must be justified. This cannot be done on the basis of 'one-offs' unless a large number of these can be assured. Investment in capital machinery is usually based on projected production quantities of products, which means that these products must be a static design for a period sufficient for the automation to be written off (using historic accounting methods).

A situation exists with automation which is similar to that described in the section on flexible machinery, where reprogramming time and the limited flexibility of most forms of automation keep a product static, only allowing manufacture of a product which is a variation of a fixed concept. It is anticipated that, within a few years, automation will become increasingly flexible and will allow the designer more freedom for dynamic designs. Changes in accounting practices may also allow the justification of automated plant to be made more easily.

11. Limited design time

As a lengthy production process tends to reinforce a product's status the same is true if only a short period is allowed for a design. Working to a very limited design time tends to encourage the designer to use existing methods, machines and components – in other words, to design a variation around a static concept.

12. Adequate time allowed for design

This is the converse of the above. A dynamic design will generally take longer than a static design, as new concepts will require longer testing to show their reliability, especially as experience cannot often be called upon. Project planning is more difficult with a dynamic design and unforeseen circumstances may arise to delay the project. Therefore if a new concept is to be considered and innovated into a marketable product adequate time must be allowed. Conversely, allowing a long period of time for a design enables the design team to investigate new concepts. This is demonstrated on Figure 4.3.

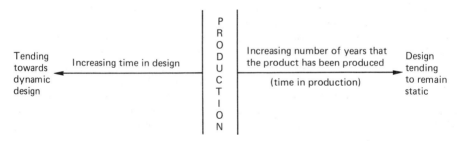

Figure 4.3 The effect of time on product status

The Concorde airliner is an example where many years were required for a 'suitable' product to be manufactured. It was first proposed at the Paris Air Show in June 1959 (Belbin, 1981), but did not enter service until 1975.

13. Insufficient design resources/management commitment

Designing new products is expensive, and seeking a new concept and then developing it into a product is generally more so than making incremental improvements to an existing design. To seek a new concept requires both management commitment to allow it to happen and sufficient resources in time, personnel and finance. If these are absent the design is likely to continue to be treated as static in a company (or may not change at all).

One company making mechanical products decided that, although the product had become dynamic, it would reduce its design department. Its management policy was to make only small changes to the existing product, maximize profits and accept the decline of the product. It had no management commitment to design. Another company in the same product area had such a commitment, and produced an effective dynamic design. However, the design team were given insufficient resources to carry the job through to fully capitalize on their new design. The design failed as a result.

The reverse situation is not so clearly marked. Adequate design resources and management commitment to design will enable new concepts to be considered but will not ensure that a dynamic design will result. These resources and commitments are still necessary to break out of a static position.

14. Restricted design
This overlaps with some of the above sections. Even with sufficient design resources and management commitment the design direction can often be limited within actual or self-imposed restrictions, which can keep a design static. Designing which depends solely upon CAD or value analysis is unlikely to be dynamic. A less serious restriction is designing a product that can be sold by the current sales force or through existing distribution systems or using production plant and equipment already in place.

15. Dominant process design
The longer a design is static, the more important becomes process design over product design. A company concentrating more of its design effort on the manufacturing process is most likely to have a static product already, or at least be treating it as static. Also it is likely to want to extend the static plateau because of the costs already incurred by the process design and the limited time spent on product design. As a result, it is less likely to seek a new concept. Petrochemical plants and the car industry are examples of industries with dominant process design.

16. Process design not dominant
If process design is limited more time is likely to be directed towards product design and there will be less potential obsolescence of manufacturing plant resulting from any dynamic design. There is, therefore, a greater incentive to produce a dynamic design.

17. Rationalization or commonality of parts between products
In an attempt to obtain economies of scale companies often try to use the same components or assemblies in a range of their products. It is currently a trend among engineering companies to rationalize as many products as possible. This limits design freedom and can make a product design continue to be static.

18. Large producers
This is similar to (7) of the macrofactors. A large company tends to benefit from economies of scale and has more dedicated machinery, which generally makes it in its interest to have a static product. It becomes less competitive when compared

with a small company when the product becomes dynamic. A large or a decreasing number of manufacturers is a sign that the product design is probably static, or is being treated as such.

19. Poor initial or continuing market research
A company that is weak in market research is more likely than one that is good at it to miss trends, variations in customer demand, technology changes or even fashion. With a greater chance of disregarding factors that could make a product design become dynamic there will be a greater likelihood of keeping the product static. Market research must be a continuous process, and not cease when the product has been designed; otherwise market changes or trends will be missed and subsequently the demand will fall below that of competitors. Such an example is a company that designed an innovative machine for the construction market. It failed to continue market research and missed the rising demand from the agricultural market that required a similar, but different, machine. As this demand came at a time of slump in the British construction market, this former market leader quickly slipped behind its better-informed competitors and never fully recovered.

20. Wide effective market research
It is only possible to detect what is happening inside one's industry (and outside it) through effective market research. If effective, factors that make a product

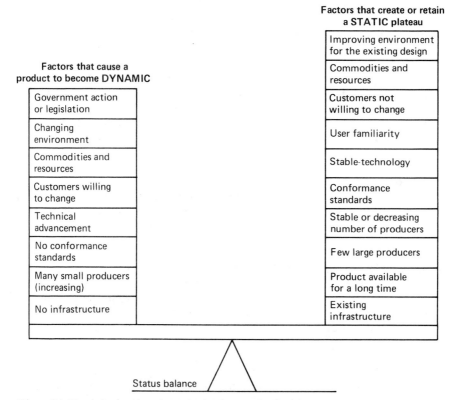

Figure 4.4 Macro factors that change/maintain a product's status

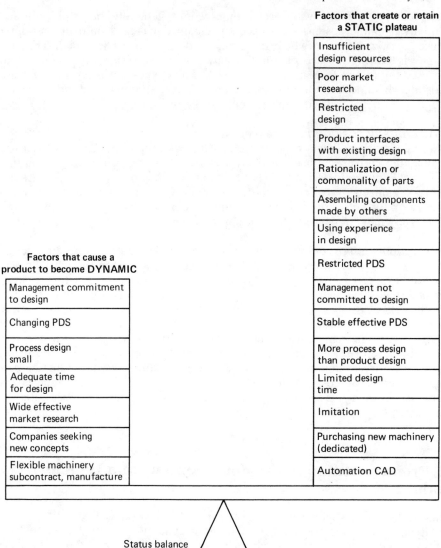

Factors that create or retain a STATIC plateau

| Insufficient design resources |
| Poor market research |
| Restricted design |
| Product interfaces with existing design |
| Rationalization or commonality of parts |
| Assembling components made by others |
| Using experience in design |
| Restricted PDS |

Factors that cause a product to become DYNAMIC

Factors that cause a product to become DYNAMIC	Factors that create or retain a STATIC plateau
Management commitment to design	Management not committed to design
Changing PDS	Stable effective PDS
Process design small	More process design than product design
Adequate time for design	Limited design time
Wide effective market research	Imitation
Companies seeking new concepts	Purchasing new machinery (dedicated)
Flexible machinery subcontract, manufacture	Automation CAD

Status balance

Figure 4.5 Micro factors that change/maintain a product's status

dynamic or keep it static can be noticed and likewise a company can detect if a product is changing status.

21. A product interfaces with or is part of an assembly made elsewhere
If a product must interface with one made by another company the manufacturer is dependent on the associated company agreeing to a change to new dynamic design. This can act against a product becoming dynamic when manufacturers of the interfacing product (who are often the purchasers) may refuse to change, or impose restrictions (e.g. demanding the same fixing holes).

This feature is more widespread than would generally be expected, and potentially dynamic designs are forced to remain unchanged until the customer produces a new design in which the dynamic design can be included. This, for example, is slowing the acceptability of new suspension systems for vehicles and has caused the failure (among other reasons) of new types of car tyres that do not fit existing wheel design. On the other hand, the easy acceptance of the alternator was due to its being a direct replacement for the dynamo.

22. A company seeking new concepts

Unless a company makes a conscious effort to seek a new concept its design will remain static. However, once it actively seeks a new concept it is not certain that an acceptable dynamic design will result, but at least it is possible. Unless they are specially organized to explore new ideas (e.g. universities), not many companies actively look for innovations, but if a company wants or needs to be innovative, it must actively make a decision to seek new concepts.

In this section we have described the factors that make or keep a product design dynamic or static, and these occur both within a company or in the marketplace. With product design in any particular market there will be factors that make it static and others that cause it to be dynamic, and these can be thought of as being on both sides of a scale (Figures 4.4 and 4.5). Generally, though, it needs more factors to make a product dynamic than to keep it static, as it is easier, cheaper and quicker to make incremental changes to an existing design than to create a new one. Therefore, for a new design to replace the existing state of the art it is usually necessary to demonstrate that there are multiple advantages for the new design in terms of cost, performance, reliability, etc. These advantages (or otherwise) become increasingly apparent as the product design specification is written.

4.5 Product status in the development of a typical product

In this section we are going to discuss the model of a product that is progressing from dynamic to static and then from static to dynamic. This will show that the effects of product status are recognizable in the development of a typical product.

Consider an innovative product introduced onto the market. The market initially will be small and therefore the producers (probably the innovators) will be few and the method of manufacture simple (little process design). The initial market will be the professional user (if it is that type of product) and the cost will be high due to the unsophisticated methods of production. The effect of 'skimming' will occur, which is the profit taking that a new product can command where few competing producers are involved. The relatively high purchase price is also due to manufacturers recouping the cost of new product development. Also, they can attract customers that some marketing literature refers to as 'innovators', people who purchase for reasons of fashion as well as improved performance. This applies mainly to consumer products. In non-consumer products the purchasing requirements tend to be made in a more rational manner, and fashion is of less importance: general performance is considered when selecting a product which best suits their needs. Another reason for the high price may simply be a function of supply and demand. A new product may not be initially available in quantities large enough to meet the demand. Of course, many innovations do not create a market: some continue with a small demand and others may be discontinued.

The market may grow. This could be due to increased demand from customers who see advantages in owning the new product or to a fall in price as manufacturers increase production and one or two decide to produce more efficiently. The lower price will bring the product within reach of a larger market and at this time generally the number of manufacturers may increase as the product becomes newly static.

This is a crucial point in the life of a design. The relative fall in price must encourage the producers to put much greater emphasis on process design. This may be done by the innovators but often it is not. Other companies which are often not innovative but are good at process design and low-cost production appear in the market and take that market from the innovators. This process is market led, which has been shown to be the most likely path to follow for product success (Part 2, ST I.4). Certain companies (often Japanese) appear to predict the supply and demand curves and create the market by taking an innovation and, by process design, reduce the price sufficiently to create a large (often consumer) market. This practice involves risk and requires effective market research. Many innovative products have been based on market prediction rather than market research, and sometimes considerable process design has been undertaken and the market has then failed to materialize. Process design reduces the unit cost/price but requires a large market.

Assuming the market exists, a static plateau occurs when production has stabilized and more process design is introduced (Part 2, ST L4B.19). This is now the peak selling period for the product. There is now a period of 'shake-out', where some manufacturers fail. It is suggested that these failures are mainly due to the manufacturers lacking or effectively harnessing static design disciplines, which may include better distribution, selling advertising, and servicing but, perhaps more importantly, lower price and product reliability. The number of manufacturers will therefore decline and the remainder will have a larger market share, which will enable them to concentrate upon process design to lower the price still further. They have to do this when a few large companies emerge in competition with each other. If any company starts producing at a lower cost level, the others, by necessity, must follow suit, decline, or re-innovate (i.e. move from the static plateau to the dynamic and produce an innovative product). This has been apparent for some years in the car industry, and all manufacturers tend to produce with the same level and type of production technology.

The smaller, failing companies may survive by concentrating on a small market segment, a specialist area or niche, or seek a new product or innovation. This suggests that large companies tend towards static products and small companies towards dynamic ones.

So much capital is often tied up in production technology, with dedicated machinery and assembly aids, that it is difficult, or uneconomic, to change the product status from static to dynamic. The longer a product has been static, the more difficult it will be to make it dynamic again. Large efficient producers may be unable to innovate if the product has been static for some years and the personnel who could innovate are no longer available. In the market, spare parts, servicing facilities and training will have become established and there will be a reluctance to upset this stability. Also, certain standards will have been set which both customers and producers will be reluctant to change (Part 2, ST L4B.13).

Therefore the larger a market grows and the longer a product design has been static, the greater will have to be the improvement of the new dynamic design, mainly in the eyes of the producer, before a product will become dynamic again. Time, relative size of the producers and market size are factors that bias a design towards remaining static.

Consider a static product that becomes dynamic again. When a product has been on the market for some period of time (say, in excess of five years) then a new product concept may appear which is a significant advance (and an improvement) on the existing design. Initially there will be a period where the new design is highly priced (as described above). Over a period of time the cost of the new product will fall, and both old and new designs will be produced in parallel, as some customers may prefer the older model or require it to interface with an existing product (e.g. Betamax tapes for an existing Sony video). The old design will become less available and will eventually be replaced by the new concept if both the products serve identical markets (except for spares replacement) or, if the product is still dynamic, by a later concept.

The manufacturer of the new concept will follow the pattern described above but those who have not started to produce the latest concept have one of three courses of action open to them. To buy into the new technology is often possible, as the established manufacturers will generally be larger than the innovators of the new concept. They could try to develop the next new technology, and, if the product is still dynamic, to 'leapfrog' over the competition. The third option is to retain their existing product, and continue to treat the product as static with a reduction of their market and an eventual decline of this product area. This third option may be forced on a company which may have a large amount of capital tied up in machinery to manufacture to the existing design, which of itself may be unsuitable for manufacturing a new product.

Furthermore, the skills required to innovate may not be available in a company which may be rich in experience with the existing concept, experience that is not immediately applicable to any new design. The company may still have an advantage in the selling and distribution systems, if this is still applicable. This was the case with dishwashers sold in traditional electrical retailers, but was not so with digital watches, which were not generally sold in jewellery shops, as were their predecessors. As has been shown, product status therefore does replicate what happens in the development of a typical product.

4.6 Product status related to the product life cycle and the S-shaped curve

As discussed above, product status can be described in simple terms as a curve. Two more familiar sets of curves are those used to describe the product life cycle and S-shaped curves that demonstrate performance improvement over time. Both have been used extensively by marketeers for many years.

4.6.1 The product life cycle (PLC)

This is one of the most popular techniques for describing the market characteristics of a product over its life. There is general agreement that products pass through

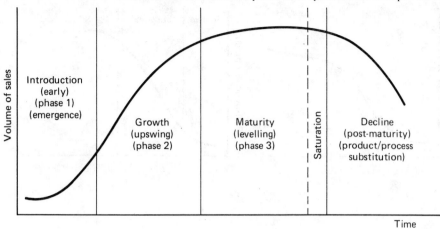

Figure 4.6 The PLC curve

four phases: introduction, growth, maturity and decline (although the terms used to describe each phase may vary). The usual shape of the PLC curve is shown in Figure 4.6.

Many writers suggest that a product's position on the PLC curve affects the management process and the structural forms of the company as well as varying the tasks needed at each phase (e.g. Hirsch, 1965; Abernathy and Utterback, 1975; Doyle, 1976; Parker, 1978; Abernathy, 1978; Cowell, 1984; Dowdy and Nikolchev, 1986). Unfortunately the general shape of the PLC curve is not consistent, and McLeod (1969), Rink and Swan (1979) and Midgley (1981) have shown a variety of shapes that occur in practice. Also Doyle (1976) has found that there is no regularity in the length of the various stages of the PLC and he quotes two extremes, one for whisky that has lasted for decades and another for hula hoops that lasted less than a year. Another failing of the PLC is that products are not left to go through the cycle from birth to death but can have their sales improved by promotion such as advertising, special offers, new packaging, price reduction, etc. For such reasons Doyle believes that the product life cycle is not a 'foundation for decision making' but is 'vacuous, empty of empirical generality and positively dangerous if used as a guide for action'. Therefore, as it stands, the PLC and the product and company characteristics that accompany it provide little benefit in product design. On the other hand, a product's position on the product status curve can be predicted. Therefore if the PLC can be related to the status curve then these product and company characteristics become usable tools in the design process.

4.6.2 The S-shaped curve

The S-shaped curve was discussed by H.G. Wells as a method for forecasting as long ago as 1902, but attempts at prediction have not been convincing as, like the PLC, the curve is prone to variation and inconsistencies. Klein (1977) described the S-shaped curve thus: 'Progress typically takes the form of rapid advance in the performance of a technology followed by a period of slower advance' (p.12). This

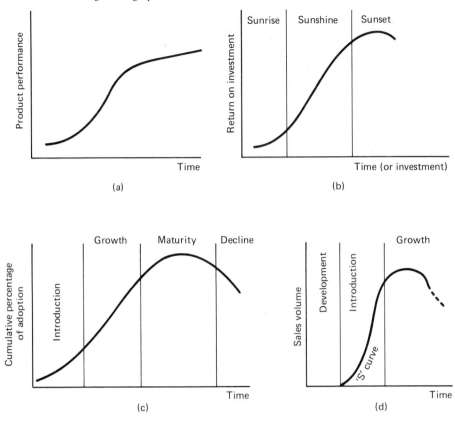

Figure 4.7 The S-shaped curve

is shown in Figure 4.7(a). Deasley (1986) shows the S-shaped curve with different axes (Figure 4.7(b)) and Parker (1978) has shown it in four parts (Figure 4.7(c)). Furthermore Nichols and Roslow (1986) show the S-curve by Fox and Wheatley (1978) in which it is compacted into the introduction and growth phases (Figure 4.7(d)). Therefore, unlike the PLC, there is inconsistency even in the accepted shape.

Nichols and Roslow (1986) have warned managers to be aware that S-curve gradients may vary as well as the time period over which they occur. When trying to relate S-curves to the design of individual products Klein (1977) is sceptical: 'Though advances can occur almost like clockwork individual advances...are unpredictable.' The S-shaped curve as described is therefore not easily used by design practitioners.

Nichols and Roslow (1986), referring to the PLC curve, note that: 'In the first three absorption stages – product introduction, market growth, and market maturity – a so-called "S-shape" curve is recognizable.' Dowdy and Nikolchev (1986) show a curve of the product life cycle which shows that a product may decline or be renewed (Figure 4.8). This renewal ties in well with Klein who, by using 'performance function' as a vertical axis, allows for products to conceptually change and improve over an indefinite period. Unfortunately, performance

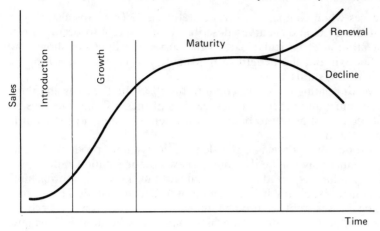

FIgure 4.8 A PLC showing decline or renewal

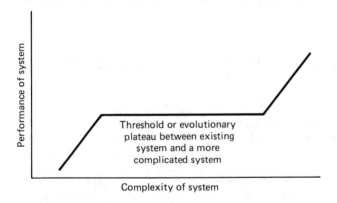

FIgure 4.9

function is an unclear measurement of product improvement, and may mean an increase (e.g. the speed of an aircraft) or a reduction (e.g. fuel consumption or weight). This being so, it is possible to compare Klein's S-shaped curve form with other S-curves and, with the 'absorption stages', with the PLC.

The declining phase of the PLC is of no interest to us, as a product at this position is probably either dynamic or potentially dynamic, and a company should not be considering designing a product with a declining demand. It should be designing the product that is to replace it, to restart the next introductory phase of the curve.

Jones (1970) has suggested that products improve in steps followed by a stable period (Figure 4.9). He also uses the 'performance of the system' as the vertical axis but has a base of 'complexity of system'. We believe that the complexity need not increase and, with certain aspects of design such as value analysis, may actually decrease.

The product status curve uses Klein's denominations of axes of performance function to a base of time. No attempt is made to measure it, and it is only used to show where a product is at any point in time. The difference, therefore, between the PLC and S-curves when compared with the status curve (which is also a type of S-curve) is that the PLC and S-curves describe what is likely to occur with a product or organization at a particular part of the curve, but does not show how this can be identified without the benefit of hindsight. The position of a product can be predicted with the status curve.

Therefore it is worth relating the status curve to the PLC and S-curves and then to read across the product and organizational features of the PLC and S-curves to show the advisable course of action to be followed when designing a product at a know position on the status curve.

The early or introductory phase is equivalent to a dynamic product. In the growth phase the product may still be dynamic or newly static (Static 1) and in the mature phase the product is on the static plateau but may be approaching conceptual vulnerability, especially if it is beginning to decline (Static 2).

The curves being inconsistent, a product may continue to grow or become mature, and the length of the mature or 'sunshine' phase may be short or long and may be followed by decline or renewal. This inconsistency highlights the strength of product status, where the curve itself is of little importance: what is important is the situation that exists within companies and the environment at that particular time.

4.7 Product status as a method for forecasting and prediction

In the previous section we described the PLC and S-shaped curves, the link between them and product status and how some have attempted to use the PLC and S-shaped curves as a method for predicting the future performance of a product in the market. Others have shown that, in the case of the PLC, there are too many exceptions to the rule, and that the basic PLC curve can be altered by many and various influences. In the case of the S-shaped curve prediction again is generally unsuccessful, due to the 'non-standard' vertical axis and the lack of rules by which the future shape of the curve can be determined. Neither advocates of the PLC or S-shaped curves have shown effectively how the problem of prediction is to be tackled in practice. The product status has the advantage over S-shaped curves and the PLC as it avoids their major weakness, time dependency. Although the status curve has a base of time it is unnecessary to consider this when using it.

Various factors that make a product status static or dynamic have been determined (Section 4.4), and these are then developed into a questionnaire in which a company may detemine the status of its own products (Design Process, Layer 3).

This essentially gives the product status at the current point in time, which is hardly prediction. However, determination of product status can highlight the areas where, if changes do occur, the product status is likely to alter. Alteration of a product status from dynamic to static or static to dynamic is all-important: 'What is of most value about the S curve is its limits' (Foster, 1986).

The product can continue to be assumed to retain its current status until the 'circumstances' alter sufficiently to change the product status. This is prediction, but must continue to be viewed periodically to detect early signs of change. Prediction is only useful if it is possible to act on it – knowing tomorrow's horse-race winners would allow one to place winning bets but knowing the world will end tomorrow does not allow much scope for individual beneficial action. Realizing that a static product has become potentially dynamic will generally allow a company to act to benefit from this new status or defend itself against competition. Knowing that a hitherto dynamic product is becoming static can again direct a company to benefit from the new status and often with sufficient prior warning to allow the company's action to be planned and implemented (e.g. reconsider an electric car if a new lightweight, high-power, low-cost battery breakthrough had been made or end development of compact disc players in the light of digital tape developments).

Product status, therefore, is not a panacea for prediction but it can be more effective than S-shaped or PLC curves in determining when changes are likely to occur and generally allowing sufficient time to plan for these changes. The direction in which these changes should be made are also described throughout this book, especially in the improved Design Process.

4.8 Do you already know your product's status?

In the research that led to the compilation of this book, when design managers were asked to consider how the design of a particular product in their range was changing (after the principle of product status had been explained to them) it was discovered that in practically every case they could identify their products as being static or dynamic. None had previously considered their products as such nor had they thought that knowing this could aid or direct their design processes. In fact, the companies generally did not treat their product design or manufacture in the best way to benefit from this knowledge of product status.

One company that previously considered its product to be static (and having had it demonstrated that it was in fact dynamic) went on to take the design 'further in the past six months than we have done in the past twenty years'.

For those who are unsure of their product's status a questionnaire has been developed that allows them to identify if their own products are static or dynamic (Design Process, Layer 3).

Part 2

There is nothing more difficult to take in hand, more perilous to conduct or more uncertain in its success than to take the lead in the introduction of a new order of things, because the innovation has for enemies all those who have done well under the old conditions and lukewarm defenders in those who may do well under the new.

Machiavelli, *The Prince*

5 The improved process of total design

The following pages describe a system for designing products up to the conceptual stage. The purpose of the system is to guide the manager or another person organizing product design through the design process in a sequential step-by-step manner, from the initial design concept right through into production.

When a product is designed disciplines are of greater or less importance at different stages of the process. This system indicates which disciplines should be emphasized or diminished so that design time can be organized and managed more effectively and therefore efficiently (i.e. the quality of product design will be maintained but the time spent on it reduced).

The system is for 'total design', and it can be used for any manufactured product, not only engineering products.

5.1 Introduction to the total design process

Previously, major studies on the management of design have concentrated on complete companies, their structure and performance, whereas the research that has led to the development of the total design process has as its genesis the companies' products. A company may have several products which may require different organization of their design. By studying a particular product these differences can be identified and highlighted. Also in the end analysis a successful product is the only useful outcome of design activity. Design without a successful product is unsuccessful design, for whatever reasons.

This system does not attempt to maximize performance in all areas of design but only those which are important in the design and manufacture of a particular product. This reduces the cost and timescale required for product design by defining and describing the organization structure best suited for that product.

The emphasis is on the early stages or 'front end' of design, as the techniques used at the subsequent stages have already been well researched and documented. The 'total design plan' has the following advantages:

1. It shows what is necessary in sequence, thereby making the work ordered and manageable (ST I.1).
2. It concentrates on the design of products, accepting that different types of product require different emphases or sets of inputs into the design process.

47

3. It indicates what disciplines are of more or less importance in the design and manufacture of products.
4. Design effort is expended in any area only when it becomes necessary, thus avoiding misdirected and wasted effort. The system shows when design effort is necessary.
5. The total design time should be reduced, enabling the product to reach the market earlier.

When first used, the system may give the impression that it takes longer than previous design processes, especially at the front end. It will be found that this more lengthy front end saves considerable time and cost in the later stages of design. Also, the information sought for any new product design may be used in subsequent models. Future versions of a similar design will only need an 'update' of the information already acquired, building upon the initial foundations established when the system was first used with the product. Therefore in subsequent designs the timescale will be considerably reduced, the effectiveness of the design will be retained and risk of failure will be minimized.

To help with its understanding, an example of the design process being used in a hypothetical company for the design of a paper clip is given in Part 3.

5.2 Overall presentation of the total design plan

The total design plan may be considered as a route map to guide the user through the design process. It takes a layered approach through a series of sequential actions, part of which is to find the product status. Completion of each layer is a suitable point at which to hold a design review (ST I.2) at which the decision to proceed to the next layer may be taken. Iteration is expected in the design plan but if the plan is being effectively operated, this should be minimal. Most of the design plan layers are at the front end of design, early in the design activity model.

Depending on the product status, the concept design stage in the design activity model may alter. For example, with a static product status new concepts will be unimportant and the design team need not look for them (ST I.3).

The design plan is shown in Figure 5.1 in outline for simplicity and to illustrate how the layers fit in with the design activity model. In Figure 5.2 the design plan is seen in more detail, showing how one would use it.

5.3 The design activity model

The design activity model gives direction to the design process. Over the past 25 years many different models have been proposed to describe the design process from market to production. These vary widely in effectiveness in describing the design process or in clarity by which the user can follow them. It is not relevant to describe their history and individual benefits or shortcomings here. However, it is necessary to illustrate and use a widely accepted design model to show the area where research has been concentrated and the effects of that research on such a model.

The design model chosen has been developed by Pugh since 1976, and a later version is shown in Figure 5.3. This model has been adopted by an increasing number of bodies (e.g. SEED – Sharing Experience in Engineering Design) and

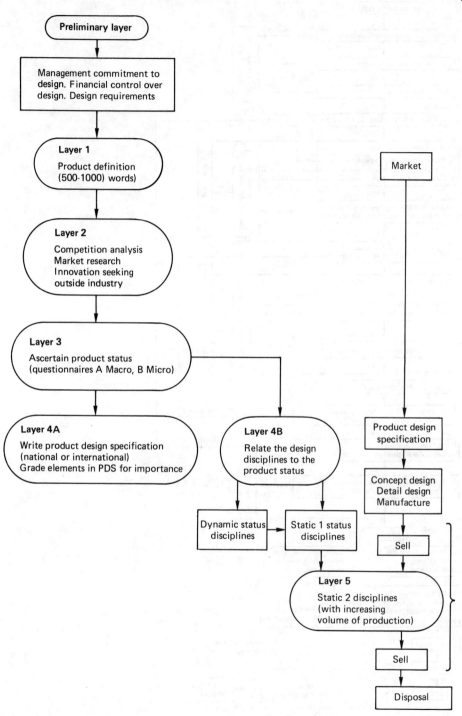

Figure 5.1 The total design plan's relationship to the design activity model

50

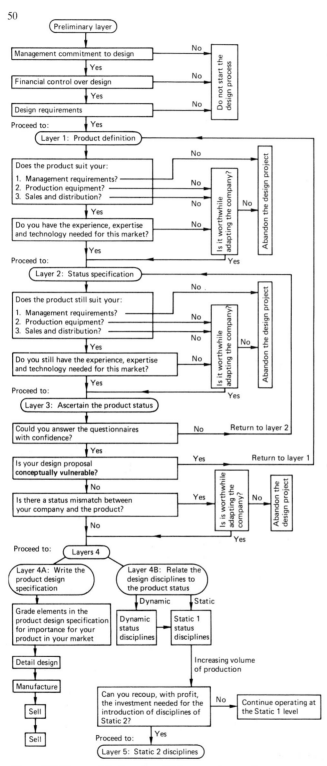

Figure 5.2 The total design plan. 'Unless you know where you are going, any road will take you there' (Levitt, 1962)

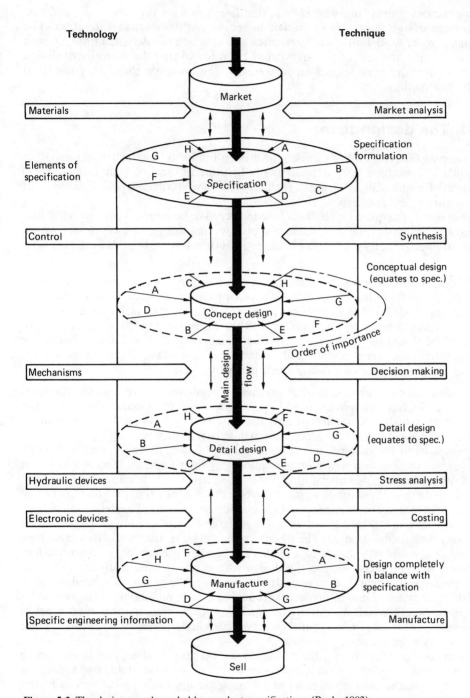

Figure 5.3 The design core bounded by product specification. (Pugh, 1982)

demonstrates simply, but with clarity, the design process for almost all products. The main design flow is from market to selling but demonstrates iteration. The design activity model provides the framework to which the designed product must relate. In this and earlier research it has been found that the majority of design models show the same sequential core stages, and these are therefore considered to be axiomatic.

5.4 The design team

In the past few years quality circles have been found to be effective in improving products. These have been defined by the Institute of Quality Assurance as 'Small groups of employees who meet regularly to solve problems and find ways of improving aspects of their work'.

In essence, the quality circle may be considered to be a process design circle that considers aspects of the manufacturing process and design of the product with a view to improving its production. Oakley (1984), referring to reviewing products, states:

> The most effective way is often to use small groups of employees drawn from different parts of the company to evaluate products and designs. For some time this approach has been increasingly used with success to tackle manufacturing problems – readers will be familiar with the term 'Quality Circle' often used to describe this group activity. There is no reason why 'Design Circles' should not operate in the same manner and, in fact, they have been for many years, but they are usually called value analysis groups (p.123).

Oakley does not expand further on these design circles. We also use the term design circle, but such groups would operate from the front end of design and not only study existing products but also the design of new ones, from the market research phase downwards through the whole design process.

Personnel in the design circle will change as the design process moves through its various stages, with new members joining as their expertise becomes relevant and others leaving. Membership of the design circle will therefore be fluid, and will include those best suited to meet the objective, which is to progress the design to the next stage. The team may include outside consultants. The design circle does not only take upon itself the task of design review, as in Oakley's terms, but also actively designs the product. The design circle will be restructured after each stage of the design and will change to a quality circle when the product is in production.

With large projects, such as the design of a car or drilling platform, there are too many people involved to operate the design circle as simply described here. With these types of design project there has to be a combination of the two styles of organization, which we call organic/mechanistic. In this, the managers meet in a design circle, as described, but then report back to their departments, which also operate as a design circle.

Some design projects may have as many as 500 people taking part in the design process, and many of these may have a contribution to make at any one time. This can be organized through a series of radiating design circles, as shown in Figure 5.4. This may radiate further into a series of smaller design circles. In effect, this makes those in the outer circles communicate with the inner circle in a mechanistic, almost traditional, pyramidal way. Unfortunately, this cannot be avoided.

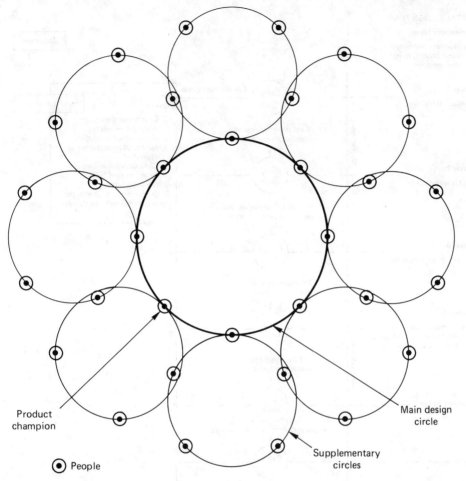

Figure 5.4 A series of radiating design circles

However, those in the outer circles are closer to personnel in the centre than they would otherwise have been in a traditional pyramid management structure. At least this means that they will, in part, be operating in an organic way (Figure 5.5).

Thus using a design circle allows a modified 'organic' design team structure (ST I.4) even in a large company. That is, all those involved will have an input into the design process, which has been found to be more effective in design. Also, communication (ST I.5) is improved but, up to now, this has been difficult to implement in a large company. This organic structure should be retained throughout the design process up to Static 2, whereupon the necessary disciplines may be thought of as a series of subcontracts within the business. In other words, each discipline is operated as a separate 'cell' receiving an input and processing it to produce an output, and this may be organized in a more mechanistic way through the use of (and constrained by) rules.

The optimum size of any such group has been determined by Schein (1969) as nine people. One person, or 'product champion' (ST I.6), should lead the group

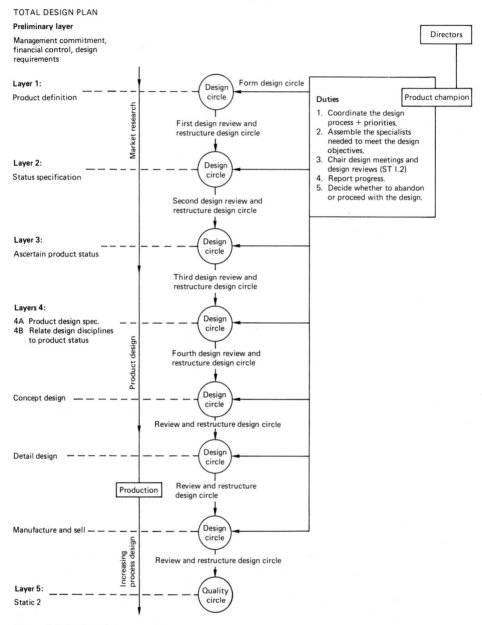

Figure 5.5 Design circles

and remain in it throughout to coordinate the design process. He or she should be someone with authority within the organization (e.g. the Design Director) or another senior person from a relevant discipline. The design circle enables the multidisciplinary nature of design to be upheld even in a large company, where otherwise the numbers involved could become unmanageable.

In the worked example of the total design process (Part 3) the structure and restructuring of a design circle as the design proceeds is shown for the manufacture of a paper clip in a hypothetical company. It will be seen that the level of seniority in the design circle tends to reduce as the design approaches production.

5.5 Project documentation

A design file should be started at the beginning of the design process and be added to as each layer is undertaken. Apart from the documentation outlined below, it will also contain various other items of information needed if an effective product design is to result (e.g. details of relevant legislation, competitors' literature, minutes of design reviews, etc.). These should be kept for the complete lifetime of the product and may be used in the case of product liability claims or to assess what design decisions were taken and for what reasons when, for example, the design of the product is updated.

5.5.1 Management requirements

This should cover, in detail, each aspect of the requirements that management wants the design to fulfil. Its length will depend on the information that is to be given and the area to which the design must be confined. These requirements should *not* be subject to revision once the design process has begun.

5.5.2 Product definition

This is as described in Chapter 8.

5.5.3 Status specification

This need only be long enough to answer the status questionnaires with accuracy and conviction. Its length will depend on the product and could be from 1000 words.

5.5.4 Status questionnaires

Apart from the questionnaires, no further documentation is required for this layer of design.

5.6 Marketing and the design plan

Levitt (1960), Peters and Waterman (1982) and Kotler (1985) all stress the importance of including the whole process if successful marketing is to be achieved. The table on page 56 itemizes marketing disciplines and where they appear in the design plan.

Place in design plan (number = layer)	Discipline (marketing vision)	
(1) Prod. defn (2) Status spec. (4A) PDS	(1) Market definition	
(2) Status spec. (4A) PDS (4A) PDS (4A) PDS	(2) Competition analysis Market analysis (3) Market segmentation (4) Prod. differentiation	Market research
(1) Prod. defn (2) Status spec. (4A) PDS (4B) Static 1 (5) Static 2	(5) Pricing	
(1) Prod. defn (2) Status spec. (4A) PDS	(6) Sales (quantity)	
(4A) PDS (4B) Static 1 (4A) PDS (4B) static 1 (4A) PDS (4B) Static 1 (1) Prod. defn (4A) PDS (4A) PDS (4B) Static 1 (4B) Static 1 (4B) Static 1	(7) Branding (8) Promotion (9) Distribution system (10) Sales personnel (11) After-sales service (12) Packaging (13) Credit policy	Marketing Mix

5.7 The quantity dilemma

When should quantity be considered in the design plan? Finding the size of a market, or market niche, is difficult. Some statistics are held for well-defined markets and certain bodies (government statistics or trade councils) supply these to manufacturers. However, for most products with small markets, market niches or new products it is not easy to obtain accurate information on market size. At some point in a product design (and therefore in some place in the design plan) the production quantity must be defined. This depends on the market size, timescale, what proportion of the total market the company is aiming at with its product and how much it can reach. A clear range must be specified so that the production methods and other services can be matched to this. Clearly, then, the quantity must be specified as one of the elements in the product design specification. But does it need to be found earlier? The purpose of the design plan is to limit action to that necessary to maximize the efficiency of the design process, and there is no need to ascertain the production quantity if it quickly becomes apparent that further design work should not continue.

In the design plan outline (Figure 5.1) the product design specification is parallel to directing the disciplines of design to the product status. As will be shown in ST L4B.1, the production volume determines whether the design effort should remain in Static 1 or proceed to Static 2. However, Static 2 is only found after the product design specification has been completed and the quantity known.

Is it necessary to find the quantity to find the status? Should the quantity be part of the status specification?

Probably an initial indication of quantity needs to be made at the outset. A vague assessment of whether the product is mass, batch or unit production in order to determine whether it is to be made in a volume that will or can suit the company's production equipment and expertise, as well as distribution, sales, etc., is useful. With an update in the design of an existing product this will be known and the company will probably be 'in phase' with the facilities needed. A company entering a new market will need to make this simple assessment which should not be time consuming. This may determine whether the company should not or cannot enter the market and further consideration of the product and its design will not continue.

To find the product status it is not necessary to know the quantity (except in relation to its price for comparison of advantages and disadvantages), and therefore this need not be included in the status specification. However, the quantity to be produced must be determined so that the production cost (and hence the selling price) can be ascertained. The competitors' selling prices can easily be found and this is part of competition analysis. Knowing this gives a range of prices and features and therefore a quick and easy determination of the product selling price and added value characteristics that will be needed if the company's new product is to be competitive. This is more difficult if a company is first in the field with a product, but generally any new design has to compete with another, even if it approaches the problem in another way (e.g. electronic versus mechanical calculators, or a new house purchase scheme against an existing mortgage system). With the 'first in the market product' the benefits of 'skimming' can be accrued, which means that a higher price may be charged than if there were many competing products (i.e. the product is less price sensitive). This means that initially the production quantities are not so vital, as there is a greater margin (profit) to play with. Of course, as more competitors enter the market the greater will be the pressure on price, and production must be more accurately geared to demand.

By then a clear determination of demand and production quantity should be apparent. Simplistically, cost price is generally proportional to the quantity produced (a stepped function): the quantity is proportional to the market demand and the market share which a company can attain. This allows us to propose the following sequence to solve the quantity problem:

1. At the start of design, as part of Layer 1 market research, determine if the production is mass, batch or unit production. This will be easily found and will show if the product is broadly suitable for the company (i.e. whether it fits the company's facilities or is worth organizing those facilities to suit the product).
2. At Layer 2 after the above, and as part of competition analysis, the prices of competitors' products can be found along with the additional cost of any special features. This is not difficult to achieve. With this knowledge it is possible to calculate, allowing for gross margins (distribution, promotion, etc.), the manufacturing cost at which a company must make the product if it is to compete.
3. Knowing this production cost, it is possible to determine more closely what type of production process will be required to be competitive. The necessary quantity will then be known as well as an approximate knowledge of the type of investment needed. At this stage it may be decided that the company cannot compete (or does not want to), and further work will cease (Layer 2).
4. The status specification can then be written if the product still appears viable, and following this the product design specification, which will investigate more closely the advantages of the new design over the competition and the value of these plus the market segment or niche that the company wishes to occupy. The price and quantity will be accurately determined in the product design specification.

We have shown that it is not necessary to decide on price and quantity until the product design specification, but before this stage some decision should be taken on approximate product quantity and on whether it is right for the company. These can be ascertained quickly and at low cost. Excessive work is avoided until after the status specification, whereupon it should be clear whether a company should proceed with the product.

The question of quantity is approached subsequently with greater thoroughness in the product design specification, where the higher costs in market research occur.

Introduction support text

I.1 The most efficient presentation of the design plan

The operations necessary in the design process can be broadly divided into five sections showing courses of action to be followed:

1. Compile the information needed to find the product status:
   market research
   competition analysis
   innovation seeking
2. Find the product status.
3. Write the product design specification.
4. Knowing the product status, emphasize the important disciplines.
5. Emphasize the disciplines necessary for all companies (regardless of product status).

Courses 1–4 can be undertaken in sequence, but time is saved without loss in quality of the design if 3 and 4 are carried out at the same time. Hence the optimum system is:

1. Compile the information needed to find the product status.
2. Find the product status.
3. Write the product design specifica-   4. Emphasize the important discipli-
   tion.   nes.

Now each of the factors that make up course 5 are considered in turn, i.e.

5. Quality and reliability, financial control and an effective sales unit.

All must be present in the company by the time the product reaches the market but some may not be important until then.

Financial control
This is important, as any aspect of design is expensive and can easily get out of control. Financial control is needed at the beginning of design and is therefore included with course 1 (see ST PL2).

Quality and reliability
This has been shown to be the most important feature in design (ST L4A.5), and as it starts at the design stage it must appear in the product design specification and continue into the selling phase.

An effective sales unit
Obviously, this is of prime importance to ensure that the product can reach the customer, and the method of selling must be considered in the product design specification. However, it may not need to be considered, or made available, before the product design specification is written. It is included at the top of Layer 4B of product design, as it is to be included whether a design is static or dynamic.

I.2 Design reviews

Design review meetings are vitally important but very expensive, as up to nine specialists at the meeting will be otherwise unproductive. It is therefore essential that design reviews are well organized and managed to be effective decision-making forums but taking up as little time as possible. The following describes how an efficient design review should operate.

The purpose of the design review is to verify that the overall requirements of the market are being fulfilled by the proposed product design meeting performance and cost specifications and also that it can be produced effectively. Reviews should be held when they are considered to be necessary and not, as some propose, only at the beginning, middle and end of the design project. They should certainly take place at the end of each design layer to discuss the results of the work carried out in the previous layer and the continuation, or otherwise, of a design. However often they are held, design reviews will achieve little if the product definition, market research, product design specification and subsequent stages of design are inadequate. The design review should be attended by everyone currently in the design circle and chaired by the product champion (see ST I.6). Where necessary, other specialists may be invited, or anyone who can make a contribution and this may even include potential customers in some cases.

There is a body of opinion that the design review should not be composed of people who are involved in the day-to-day design of the product (including the chairman/product champion), but we believe that those who are actually involved in the design will have a greater understanding of the topic, and should therefore have sufficient authority to take the necessary decisions. In any case, in a small company there may not be the number of experts to make up a second group of uninvolved specialists to undertake the review. Using people who are actively interested in the design does present difficulties with impartiality and objectivity. At the design review members of the design circle should set aside any preconceived opinions and personal preference and make judgements only on the evidence presented at the meeting. Members must note that the purpose of the design review is to make decisions that will benefit the product's smooth progress to being a successful product in the market, which will benefit the organization and, eventually, themselves. Therefore a design review should not be considered as a chance to 'win points' or, conversely, individuals should not show undue sensitivity to difficult probing questions. Strong chairmanship by the product champion can prevent the meeting deteriorating into a 'slanging match'.

When the product design specification has been written the design review will take place after each stage of the design activity model has been completed or before any major investment decision that may be difficult to reverse. The main topics of discussion will be the work completed with reference to the PDS (Figure 6.3 may be used as a checklist) and changes in priority in relation to other company design projects should be announced at design reviews. The review should not be used for concept generation or any other creative activity, and certainly not to direct the subsequent design: the purpose of the design review is to refine the product design.

A typical design review will have the following format. The product champion will give a formal introduction and state what documents each member of the design circle present should have received (which will have included an agenda of the meeting). Those responsible for various aspects under consideration will then present a short verbal report and this will be followed by a discussion in which questioning must be encouraged. Decisions will then be taken. This may be a call for action by someone (who should be identified) and a date agreed for completion of the point of action. Ideally,the next point on the agenda should not be started until a decision has been taken and recorded. The authors have attended too many meetings where the only decision taken is to re-discuss the point at the next meeting: this should be avoided.

For the purpose of understanding what decisions were taken (and why they were taken) a secretary should record the minutes of each meeting, which should include calls for action, decisions and recommendations. The secretary should also collect and distribute the agenda and necessary information to those attendiing the meeting, preferably a full week before the review so that all will have the opportunity of assimilating the data. The agenda should state at least the date, location and time of the start and proposed finish of the meeting. It should include a list of the names of all those participating as well as decisions that need to be taken to help focus the minds of those involved on important areas. The secretary (who should not be a member of the design circle) will also be needed after the review to follow up the agreed points of action. Documentation after the design review should inclulde the following:

1. A record of follow-up action;
2. A record of how the design proceeded – this will help with the 'topping-up' process that can be used for any subsequent design of the product;
3. Legal back-up for use in design protection or cases of product liability. The documentation must therefore be retained almost permanently and certainly while the product is still on sale or in use.

The design review meetings should continue after the product goes on sale and throughout the sales life of the product.

A design review does not design anything and cannot be a substitute for good design practice throughout other areas of the design process, but if well planned, organized, controlled, documented and reported it can increase confidence in the eventual success of the product.

I.3 Product status in relation to the design activity model

The area covered by this book is concentrated at the top end of the market down but stopping before the detail design stage. However, defining the disciplines that accompany a product of a particular status means that parts of the subsequent stages are also relevant. The subsequent improved design process 'stretches' this model between the market and specification stages by including various layered procedures at the low-cost front end of design.

Further, identification of the product status showing a static product will indicate that concept design is of much less importance as the basic concept is unlikely to alter, although consideration of subconcepts in component parts may be important (the status of these components will need to be identified in some products). When a design model is referred to in the text the model is the one shown in Figure 5.3.

I.4 Organic and mechanistic structures

These terms were first used by Burns and Stalker (1961), who found that the 'organic' system was best suited to conditions of change or unstable conditions.

In the mechanistic system the problems can be broken down into specialisms 'as if it were the subject of a subcontract' and direction is by formal rules typified by a pyramidal type of communication and organizational chart.

The organic system has a more 'lateral' type of communication and 'tends to resemble lateral consultation rather than vertical command'. As design, by its very nature, involves constant change it would appear that an organic system should be proposed throughout and all should be involved. However, as was said in one large company, 'If everybody had a say in design nothing would get done'. This valid argument has been answered by the proposal for a 'design circle', which is described and discussed above.

Ansoff and Stewart (1967) state that:

with rapid technological advance or an unstable market ... This demands an organizational structure which fosters a high degree of technology transfer and interaction with marketing. In a mature industry with a long product life cycle these organizational objectives are less important ... and it is possible for a project to move from one stage to the next along a well defined path without the close association between research and development, production and marketing.

This suggests that the mechanistic system may be better suited to truly static design, and this theme is restated by The Design Council (1985): 'The organic mode seems best suited to the early creative stages of the innovation process, while the mechanistic mode fits well at the manufacturing, distribution and service stages where formal, set patterns of action are needed.' Both these statements ignore the effectiveness of quality circles. Herriot (1985) observed that 'The prediction would therefore be that the more subject to change an area of technology is, the more flexible both the internal technical systems and the roles associated with them will be'.

It has been found that the more change in the technology and the market, the less formal was the organizational structure (Lawrence and Lorsch, 1967). There was more communication between individuals at the same level of responsibility, more delegation of authority and less clearly defined roles. Lawrence and Lorsch also found that where the environment was 'steady' (e.g. in the manufacture of containers) there was a more formal structure which was found to be more effective.

Woodward (1965), two years earlier, had written about the differing types of 'role structure' in unit/branch, mass and process industries. Noting that in mass production the heavy investment in plant made major changes in product difficult, she observed that these types of organization delegated authority less and had more rules than the other two types. In other words, they become more mechanistic as they produce at the static level.

Parker (1982) describes the company organization which accompanies 'positional' (static) companies and 'innovative' (dynamic) ones. He states that for positional companies 'The company organization, not unnaturally, tends to be impersonal, heirarchical and status dependent', and for innovative companies 'The organization pattern is likely to have the character of a dual structure, a vertical one based on a specialized function and a horizontal one concerned with co-ordinating independent activities.' Our recommendations are not dissimilar. Nyström (1979), Johne and Snelson (1988), Takeuchi and Nanaka (1986) and Cooper (1984) all confirm the findings of Burns and Stalker.

It appears, therefore, that the mechanistic structure is more effective, faster and easier to operate where change is limited; otherwise it is less effective and the organic is more effective, even though it may be more difficult to operate. It has also been shown in some studies that the organic system is also more popular with workers (Fullan, 1970). As process design is similar in its nature to product design, the organic system is considered appropriate for both. The mechanistic system, therefore, may not be suitable in most design situations but may become more effective at the latter part of Static Levels 1 and 2. The design process will become more mechanistic as the design becomes increasingly static.

The danger to companies organized mechanistically for static products is their inability to respond when and if the product becomes dynamic again, which is occurring much more frequently as companies adopt more systematic, searching and rigorous design procedures. At the point of response, the company has still the same people in post who have had to become used to the security of the mechanistic structure – people cannot change overnight. The difficulty therefore may be summarized as recognition and response.

I.5 Communication

Good communication between members of the design team and outside bodies has been found to be important to obtain the necessary information needed in design. In *Innovation: A Study of the Problems and Benefits of Product Innovation* (The Design Council, 1985) it is stated that 'Firms that innovate successfully are generally also successful in establishing internal and external communication networks'. Alexander (1985) has noted: 'Innovative design does not sell itself but that it depends on the creative communications skills and positive commitment of marketing staff working in conjunction with designers to ensure the commercial success of a product.'

In his paper, which brings together the findings of research on what makes a new product a success, Cooper (1983) provides six 'lessons' for new product design. Included in these is 'internal communication and coordination between internal groups greatly fosters successful innovation'. Cooper points to the multidisciplinary nature of the new product process and these 'multiple' inputs must be coordinated and integrated throughout the process.

The need to structure the design process to improve communications has been considered by the authors and is one of the factors that has led to the proposal for organizing design team members into 'design circles'.

1.6 Product champions

With a floating membership of the design circle, there must be one person that is a permanent member to give consistency and continuity to the meetings – a 'product champion'. The idea of a product champion has been shown to be beneficial in several studies and is one of the few features that has escaped with credit from the idea of Venture Groups, an area that was popular some years back but which is now in decline. The product champion should lead and remain in the design circle throughout the design project to coordinate the entire process, and should be someone with authority within the organization, such as the Design Director, or another senior person from a relevant discipline who understands the design process.

It is vital that the product champion is kept informed of any management decision that affects the design project such as changing the project priority in relation to any other design projects in the company.

The need for one or a few people committed to a design project has been described in the literature. Twiss (1980) states that 'Research into the causes of success and failure in technological innovation reveals the frequent presence of a number of factors . . . The most critical of these factors is: (7) Commitment by one or a few individuals'. The Design Council (1985) says:

> (7) Key individuals. Successful innovation is associated with the presence in the firm of one or more 'key individuals' (product champions, technical innovators, business innovators) . . . To be fully effective, the key individual needs sufficient authority.

Peters and Waterman (1982) and Kanter (1983) also list the presence of a product champion as being important in the success of new products. Rubenstein *et al.* (1976) found 54 facilitators for success in their study of American products, among the most important being 'the existence of a strong product champion'. The case for a product champion has been well made and we include the need for one in the improved design process.

6 A system for total design management of products

Preliminary layer: before design begins

Before a company embarks on designing a new product certain characteristics and disciplines must be present. The *management* of the company must have a *commitment* to the design of the product, which generally means that *direction* and *approval* of design must come from the top (ST PL 1). This is the overriding constraint of the whole design process. Additionally, having a common view of just what design is in their company and having this view disseminated throughout the company will add effectiveness to that commitment.

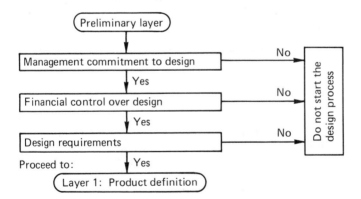

There must also be *financial control* over the process, since design of products is expensive and such control is essential if the necessary return is to be obtained (ST I.1 and ST PL 2). Sufficient funds must also be available to ensure that the design process can be completed and design should not start if they are not available. The design process as described (and if followed) will ensure that funds will be directed towards the most important areas and disciplines so that maximum value for money will be obtained. Also, through product status, the disciplines that can be decreased are described, which will lead to further efficient use of funds. The total design plan provides a measure of control during the design process and of financial planning at the outset of design.

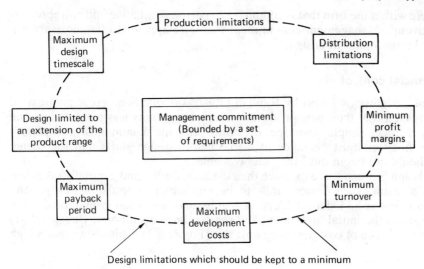

Figure 6.1 An example of possible design requirements. The more requirements imposed on the design, the more likely it is that the product will be a static design. Beware of concept vulnerability brought about by too many management requirements

Management commitment and financial control will probably take the form of a set of *requirements* which the product must meet. These may include a timescale for the product to reach the market, turnover expected, maximum development costs or some other factor with which the product must comply (production, distribution, etc.) (see Figure 6.1). This provides the *design boundary*. Having achieved management commitment to the design, financial control and a set of requirements, the product to be designed should now be defined as described in Layer 1 after forming the design circle.

First design review (ST I.2)

Preliminary layer support text

PL 1 Management commitment

Management commitment was found to be necessary for successful innovation in Project Sappho. Rothwell *et al.* (1972) observed that 'The responsible individuals in the successful attempts are usually more senior and have greater authority than their counterparts who fail'. Twiss (1980) found that 'Research into the causes of success and failure in technological innovation reveals the frequent presence of a number of factors', and among the most critical he includes '(2) Reference to the organization's corporate objectives' and '(6) An organization receptive to innovation'.

If a design project is outside corporate objectives it is unlikely to have management commitment. Where innovation is necessary, again management must be receptive to or committed to innovating. Rothwell (1977) states that 'Successful innovators are associated with . . . . top management creating an atmosphere within the firm that is conducive to personal initiative and entrepreneurial endeavour'. Management commitment therefore appears to be necessary if a firm is to be successful in design.

PL 2 Financial control

One of the conclusions found by Randall (1980) was that 'The great majority of respondents felt that their new product development activity was restricted by one or more factors: simple shortage of funds was the commonest complaint'. Adequate finances must be made available before design starts and the design process should not begin until they are available.

Static design is much less expensive than dynamic design and generally takes less time. As a result, such design tends to be much more popular with company accountants, banks and shareholders. A highly innovative design may take many years to recoup the initial investment and reach a breakeven point. Buggie (1981) shows a typical cure of cost design against this (Figure 6.2). This shows that a high

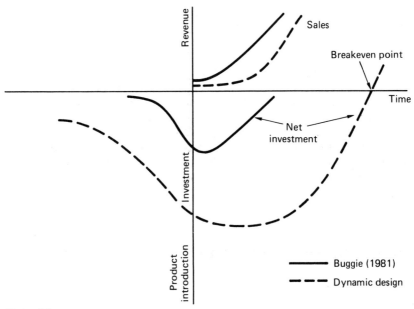

Figure 6.2

investment needs to be made before the product is placed onto the market and that a period of rising sales is needed before the new product becomes profitable.

In Figure 6.2 we have developed Buggie's diagram to show that a dynamic design will require a greater amount of investment and will take longer for a profit to be made. Linked with this is the greater risk factor generally associated with dynamic design.

Many products do not become profitable. The overall success and survival of a company often depends on the profitability of a few products whose success must recoup not only the investment made in their design but also that made in new product failures. This arrangement has been taken further by Starr (1963), who says: 'A company which fails with a new product must consider not only the lost investment, but also the cost of lost opportunities due to not having used that investment in another way'.

As a result it is often not possible to persuade financial institutions that they will get an adequate return on their capital and that they must be prepared to wait longer for it. Shareholders require an annual dividend and can be seen to invest for short-term gain. The situation is different in Japan, where the government is prepared to make loans to industry and does not expect a return for up to 10 years. Innovation is therefore a less risky proposition to companies in Japan than it is in Europe or the United States. Listed companies, which have a responsibility to their shareholders, are less likely to become involved in designing products that are innovative designs unless they can offset the cost of these against the returns generated from existing products. This may be another reason why small companies, which may not be listed on the Stock Exchange, are more innovative than the larger companies which are. For successful design financial planning and control must precede new product planning and control in order to ensure that the probability of success justifies the necessary capital outlay.

Layer 1: product definition

Now we must define precisely what the product is to be. This will allow us to state what the competition is and at what market it is to be aimed, enabling subsequent competition analysis and finding the product status. (This is explained by an example in Part 3, using the Sinclair C5 electric car.)

Product definition sets the direction for the whole subsequent design process and is a major element in the design plan. The definition must be for a product and

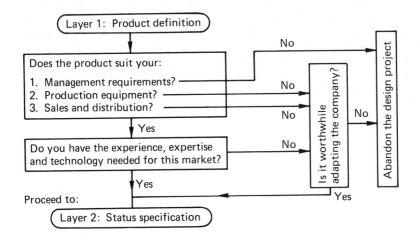

not for a company's course of action. For example, it may be a very narrow definition such as a 'rotary distributor fuel injection pump' or, covering a wider area, a 'new fuel injection pump', but it must not be a 'pumping apparatus'. This is too vague a definition, as it does not define a product as such, and therefore competition analysis cannot be undertaken. The narrow product definition will be shown at the 'ascertain the product status' stage (Layer 3) of the design plan if the product definition is too narrow and therefore perhaps conceptually vulnerable. If at that stage it is shown not to be conceptually vulnerable the subsequent design process will be easier.

The choice of product to be designed may come from various sources (ST L1.1). The source is unimportant, as the subsequent stages of the design plan will be the same for all products, although product proposals as a result of market pull (ST L1.2) are likely to be more successful than those eminating from technology push (ST L1.3).

The product definition should state:

1. The product title.
2. What purpose the product is to perform.
3. Against what type of product it will be competing.
4. What market it will serve.
5. What it is to do.
6. The anticipated performance.
7. The competitors.

8. Why there is a need.
9. The anticipated demand/price.

Five hundred words should be the minimum length of the product definition: significantly more than this is probably not necessary as it is only a description from which the design process (but not the design) can start. It is similar to what some people call a design brief or feasibility study: it is *not* a status specification or a product design specification.

Educated guesses can be allowed in the product definition (for example, anticipated demand and price); even though these are not likely to be very accurate, they will aid the understanding of the product design under consideration and will lay the foundation for the information which will subsequently be refined and expanded in subsequent stages of the design plan. No special disciplines are required to compile this layer.

Note. At this stage management will need to give a priority for the design project in relation to any other design projects being carried out in the company. This priority must be given to the product champion and updated if priorities change and the product champion must inform the design circle of changes in priority at design reviews. The need to assign priority is necessary when a company has more than one product design project which will call on the same services such as tool room, prototype manufacture and drawing office time.

First design review (see Appendix 2)

1. Does the project meet your management requirements?
2. Does the anticipated demand suit the company's production equipment, distribution system, sales, etc.?
3. Do you have, or can you obtain, the necessary experience and expertise in this market?
4. Is the technology within your reach?

If you cannot meet these criteria you should abandon the design project. If you can, proceed to Layer 2.

Layer 1 support text

L1.1 Sources for new product design

A new product can originate from four basic 'triggers':

1. *Market pull.* This is the identification of an existing customer need from strong external pressures such as fashion, competition, legislation, seasonal factors, etc. as a result of market research. This is the most successful source of new products. The need is identified before starting the project (ST L1.2).
2. *Technology push.* This is the recognition of a new technical potential such as a research finding. These types of products are most widely heralded and may appear on BBC TV's *Tomorrow's World*. Unfortunately, they are usually unsuccessful. It is still necessary to identify a market need for a technology-push product before proceeding with the design. Admittedly, this may be more

difficult in some cases where potential users may not be able to appreciate the capabilities of something completely new. This difficulty should not be used as an excuse for not attempting to find if it fulfils a customer need. Most technology-push products do serve a market which is currently occupied by a similar product, and therefore although the technology may be new, many of the market opportunities will not (ST L1.3).

3. *Situation opportunity.* This may occur, for example, when existing tooling has worn out and a new design may be undertaken to take advantage of the latest manufacturing methods. This is hardly likely to make a great impact on sales but the market may have a preference for the newer design if the change is visible.

4. *Direct request.* This trigger must be treated with caution. If the request comes from a very large organization such as the Ministry of Defence, Marks and Spencer, Ford etc. it should be worthwhile. Most direct requests originate from existing customers and may only be for that customer. As a rule of thumb, if the company making the request is not large, discover whether there are likely to be other customers before embarking on the design.

The total design process will handle all these types of new product. Any fear that a company is becoming too 'production oriented' with its design proposals does not matter as, acting on the subsequent market orientation of the design process, unsuitable designs will be eliminated.

L1.2 Market pull

Rothwell (1985) states:

The majority of successful innovations arise in response to the recognition of a need of one sort or another (need pull), as opposed to the recognition of a new technical potential (technology push). Where a new technical potential does become available first (which occurs most frequently in the case of the more radical innovation) successful innovators determine that the need exists before they proceed with the project.

Randall (1980) maintains that 'A common theme of almost all the studies is the crucial necessity of establishing that there is an actual or potential market demand for the product'. Further importance of market research to ascertain market pull is described in ST L2.2.

L1.3 Technology push

Technology push is the opposite of market pull. Many dynamic designs are achieved through technology push, and therefore it is associated with, and is an indication of, dynamic design. Conversely, too much reliance on market pull can result in low-risk products and imitation at the expense of innovation. This is explained by Hayes and Abernathy (1980): 'Uncertainty is least when extension of an existing product range is at hand and is greatest when innovation is undertaken.

This makes innovation unpopular with management since neither design nor marketing can quantify the situation'.

	High		*Low*	
	←	Risk	→	
	←	Cost	→	
Technology push	←	Return	→	Market pull
	←	Time	→	
	←	Effect on the company	→	

Layer 2: Status specification

The status specification is a brief written document compiled after an investigation into certain aspects of the product, knowledge of which is needed so that the product status can be found. Our research showed that certain characteristics and disciplines are necessary in all companies, whatever the product status, and these need to be present in a company before product status can be considered to any effect.

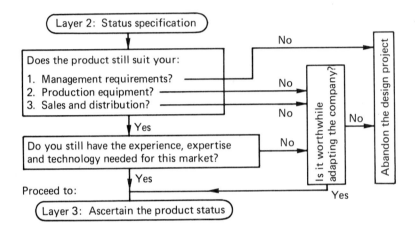

It was also discovered that there existed certain marketwide features helpful in determining the status of a product (Macro) as well as company characteristics which were best suited for dealing with that product status (Micro). It is necessary to match the product status in the market to that adopted in a company to optimize design effort and resources.

The status specification is needed so that the Macro and Micro questionnaires of Layer 3 can be answered. Whatever the product status, it is necessary to undertake the following:

1. *Competition analysis*
   Pricing/quantity (Introduction).
   Number and size of competitors (quantity).
   Product features. Advantages and disadvantages (Layer 3).
2. *Market research* (ST L2.1)
   Relevant legislation.
   Relevant economic information.
   Relevant resources.
   Relevant standards.
   Infrastructure around current product (e.g. fuel, spares, servicing, distribution, selling, skills, etc.).
3. *Innovation seeking outside your industry* (ST L2.2)
   Technical changes that may be used in your design or be a threat to the concept, product or market.
   Analogous products.

The depth of the investigation need only be sufficient to answer the status questionnaires with confidence. This information will be used again in the product design specification, where investigations into the market, competition and technology will be made in much greater depth.

Type of information needed and possible sources

1. Competition analysis
Product features, advantages and disadvantages, pricing, strengths and weaknesses, number and approximate market share of competitors, who and what are the competition. Use: Catalogues, exhibitions, user comments, questionnaires (not needed at this stage: purchasing analysis, parametric analysis (ST L4A.4), matrix analysis).

2. Market research (ST L2.1)
Politics and legislation. Laws and government policy. Use: Newspapers and magazines (not needed at this stage: details from government departments).

Standards. Conformance standards, custom and practice, user familiarity. Use: User comments and market research.

Infrastructure. Fuel, spares, servicing, distribution, selling, skills. Use: User comments and market research.

Economic climate. Resources (scarcity and glut), relative prices between major components user in or with the product. Use: Newspapers, magazines, catalogues (not needed at this stage: long- and short-wave analysis).

Safety legislation. Use: ROSPA or Health and Safety Executive.

3. Innovation seeking outside your industry
Advantages and disadvantages of new innovations that may be used with, or replace, the existing product. Use: Magazines, exhibitions (not needed at this stage: patent searches).

Not knowing the approximate price and production quantity, is this product still right for your management requirements and company's production, expertise, distribution and sales? If it is, proceed to Layer 3 of the design plan. If not, are you able to (or do you want to) change to make your company suitable for the product? If not, abandon the design project.

Second design review (ST I.2)

Layer 2 support text

L2.1 Market research and product status

A vital part of the design process is marketing and the link between market research and product design. Market research provides the inputs to most of the elements of the product design specification and therefore the quality of market research is directly related to the likelihood of success for the new product design. This is described by Blois and Cowell (1973): 'While marketing research cannot eliminate risk, it can however reduce it and perhaps improve the quality of decisions particularly by removing errors made where decisions are based on feel and intuition alone' (p.3).

However, a survey by the Institute of Marketing with the University of Bradford, and reported in *The Times* Special Report (31 May 1985), discovered that:

Only half the industrial goods firms that responded conducted market research, compared with four-fifths of the fast-moving consumer goods companies. Only 36% of the 2000 companies surveyed carried out formal market research in the sense of commissioning a market research agency.

Cooper (1976) describes the folly of ignoring market research.

The main reasons for [design] failure were found to be a lack of understanding of customers, competition, and market environment . . . A lack of marketing research personnel and skills was thought to have contributed more to industrial product failure than any other resource deficiency.

Rothwell *et al.* (1972) listed the following among the features for success:

(1) Successful innovators were seen to have much better understanding of user needs.
(2) Successful innovators pay more attention to marketing.

Twiss (1980) shows that this is not only a British problem: 'There is substantial evidence from both sides of the Atlantic that market orientation is still woefully absent in major decisions and that this is the major source of failure.'

The Centre for the Study of Industrial Innovation (1971) found that the most common reason for research and development project abandonment was 'apparently unfavourable market characteristics which arose, or were only identified by the firm, after development costs had been incurred'.

These writers have demonstrated and emphasized the importance of market research to successful product design. We also have identified poor market research (along with a poor PDS) as being one of the main weaknesses.

Corfield (1979) has listed what the design input should include:

1. Establish the market size.
2. Conduct preliminary saleability/marketability evaluation.
3. Determine the customer requirement.
4. Establish the required customer specification.
5. Determine product selling price to be competitive.
6. Conduct price performance evaluation.

Marketing entails more than only market research: it also comprises the '4Ps' – product, price, promotion and place (see Part 1, Section 2.4). Therefore it also includes the selling end of the design process, i.e. selling methods, distribution, advertising and promotion, branding, pricing, sales personnel, after-sales service, packaging and credit policy.

In the context of product status, the importance attributed to marketing can be seen in the recommendation that several marketing disciplines are deemed to be necessary for all companies, regardless of their product status. Even when market research is not investigating a market for a particular product it should be looking at the competition or at new technology. This ensures that existing products remain competitive: where they are not, this shortfall can be identified and design improvements made.

L2.2 Innovation seeking outside industry

One of the factors found to be present for success in project Sappho (Rothwell *et al.*, 1972) was that 'Successful innovators made more effective use of outside technology and outside advice, even though they perform more of the work in house'. Klein (1977) observed that, of fifty key inventions of this century, none came from a major firm in the industry – most were by small inventors. These findings have been more recently confirmed by Stolte-Heiskanen's (1980) study of fifty research laboratories.

Thackray (1983) has also noted that 'There is no prescribed rate of progress; instead it occurs in sudden unpredictable spurts, often from unlikely sources'. Part of the aim of this research is to make these 'spurts' more predictable, but the message that comes across is that it is necessary to seek these changes outside one's own industry. The Design Council (1985) also states that 'Firms that innovate successfully . . . make deliberate efforts to survey useful ideas generated outside the firm'. Rothwell (1985) observed that:

It appears that new firms, initially, are better adapted to exploit new techno-market regimes, breaking out from existing regimes within which established corporations, for historical, cultural and institutional reasons, might be rather strongly bound. Today we can see how the 'New Wave' biotechnology industry is being pioneered in the USA by new small firms.

Nelson (1984) also highlights the importance of surveying the whole scene:

These sharp shifts in technological regimes often were masked by changes in the nature of the predominant companies . . . with the advent of the integrated circuit, the old electronic equipment producers, like General Electric and Westinghouse, failed to stay competitive and were replaced as technological leaders by such companies as Texas Instruments and Intel.

The above comments demonstrate the importance of looking outside one's own industry to detect changes which may make a product dynamic.

As mentioned earlier, new technology is one of the commonest causes for otherwise healthy products to be superseded, but do you search for new technology that may affect your products? When we asked design managers how they kept informed of new technology we were told that they read trade magazines and visited trade exhibitions. This is a blinkered way of seeking technological change.

Most companies look no further than their immediate competitors and spend most of their energy imitating them, often to miss out on the major changes that are taking place just outside their field of view. It is essential to look far wider than your own market if you are to identify possible threats or opportunities.

	Yes (static)	No (dynamic)
Questionnaire A Macro: Starting a new product design *Product type under consideration:* *Comparison with which product:*		
1. If there has not been any technical advance recently that may be used to replace this product, tick the 'Yes' column and go on to Question 6. If there has, name it and tick the 'No' column.		
2. Is there a large infrastructure based on the existing design that *cannot* be used with the new design (e.g. fuel, sales, spares, distribution, servicing, skills etc.)? Give one tick in the 'Yes' column for each, or one tick in the 'No' column if there are none.		
3. Are there any conformance standards for this product that cannot be met by the new design?		
4. Put a tick in the 'No' column for every *two* advantages of the technical advance that would make a customer change from the existing product (one tick for lower price). (Think ahead. Could investment in the manufacturing process make the technical advance cheaper than the current product?)		
5. Put one tick in the 'Yes' column for every *two* disadvantages that would make a customer prefer the existing product.		
6. Are a few relatively large companies dominating this product market? Tick the 'No' column if any technical advance mentioned in Question 1 comes from one of these companies.		
7. Do most companies making this product appear to to copy each other?		
8. Has the product been available in its present form for more than five years?		
9. Tick the 'Yes' column if the number of your competitors is decreasing or remaining the same, tick the 'No' column if it has increased.		
10. Recently there may have been changes in the economic climate, legislation or resources that make the existing product more (or less) viable to customers. Tick the 'Yes' column if these changes have made the existing product more viable or attractive to customers. Tick the 'No' column if these changes have made the existing product less viable or attractive to customers. (If neither, leave blank.)		
Total:		
Judgement:		

Advantages or disadvantages of one design over another as perceived by a customer

For use with Questionnaire A Macro

1. Greater quality and reliability.
2. Demonstrably safer.
3. Easier maintenance.
4. Easier to use (ergonomics).
5. Lower price.
6. Stronger (more robust, longer lasting).

(1–6 are of greater importance, but relative importance may vary, depending on the type of product and market – ST L4A.3 and L4A.5)

7. Performance:
   (a) More accurate;
   (b) Faster;
   (c) More range;
   (d) Greater load;
   (e) Quieter;
   (f) More economical – lower running costs
                        – lower energy use
                        – less effort;
   (g) Less pollution;
   (h) More 'add-on' useful features;
   (i) Wider environmental use (or better protection from the environment);
   (j) Less interference;
   (k) Longer shelf life;
   (l) Longer life in use (or corrosion resistance).
8. Physical features:
   (a) Smaller/larger;
   (b) Lighter;
   (c) More convenient (parking, storage);
   (d) Easier to install;
   (e) Easier to obtain;
   (f) More stable.
9. Aesthetics:
   (a) Better appearance;
   (b) Better finish;
   (c) More comfortable;
   (d) Higher status – esteem
                     – fashion
                     – image.
10. Environment:
   (a) Less/easier legislation;
   (b) Less tax, insurance, etc.

Note This list is not exhaustive.

Questionnaire B Micro: New product or updating an existing product

Product name:

	Yes (static)	No (dynamic)
1. Does this product interface with other products or fit an assembly not made by your company?		
*2. Do you/will you use much dedicated machinery or automation in the manufacture of this product?		
*3. Do you/will you use CAD for the design of this product?		
*4. Does your company have a greater market share or turnover than most of your competitors (or potential competitors)?		
†5. Is a fast design time one of the three most important considerations when embarking on a new design?		
†6. Must new designs use the existing sales force and/or distribution networks?		
†7. Must new designs use the existing production facilities?		
†8. Must tried and proven methods be used in the design of new products?		
†9. Must new designs be an extension of the existing product range?		
10. Is this product made by assembling components the majority of which are made by other companies?		
11. Is more process design done than product design? (Design of the production method rather than of the product.)		
12. Has the product design specification remained significantly unaltered recently by your market research department and by your main customers?		
13. Do you use the same components from this product in several other products?		
Total		

*If a 'Yes' answer is given to these questions it is in your company's interest to seek static products.

†'Yes' answers to these questions suggest that your company is restricting design to static design. Is this necessary or sensible?

Layer 3: Ascertain product status

The status questionnaire is one of the most important parts of design, as the results obtained from it direct the user through the subsequent design process.

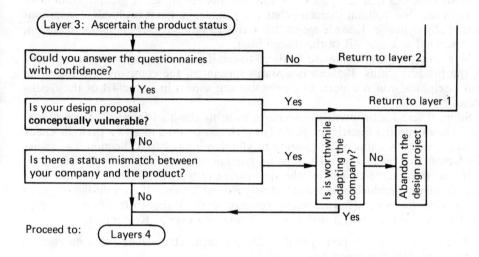

The status questionnaires

A series of factors have been determined that make a product static or dynamic (see Section 4.4) and are divided into micro and macro. Micro factors are those existing within a company and therefore can be controlled by that company, whereas macro factors are those outside the control of a company and exist in the market and its environment. These factors have been compiled into two questionnaires which can now be used to determine the status of the product in the market (macro questionnaire) and to show the status the product is being assigned in the company (micro questionnaire).

Initially it will appear that these two questionnaires can be quickly and easily answered. This is certainly the case, but to answer them accurately you will need to fully understand your product, company and market as well as the environment in which your company operates. Users have commented on the brevity of the questionnaires but have been unable to identify or justify additional questions.

Before the questionnaire was shown to potential users it was retrofitted to various products within certain time frames so that the benefit of hindsight could be used (e.g. the design of the pocket calculator in 1963, work-holding equipment, safety interlocks, car alternators *vs* dynamos, the digital watch in 1970, cars in 1980, etc.). The effect of this retrofitting was to cause some changes of balance but few of content.

Using the information compiled in Layer 2 the status questionnaires should now be answered to determine the status, static or dynamic, of the product that is being designed. To find the status of the product, Questionnaire *A Macro* should be answered, and to assist with this some possible product advantages and disadvantages are shown. It is also helpful and necessary to ascertain whether yours is a static or dynamic company and to see if your company's status is 'in tune' or mismatched with the product that is to be designed. A mismatch may indicate that the product under consideration is unsuitable for your company. To find the status of your company, Questionnaire *B Micro* should be answered.

An equal number of ticks in both columns or a majority of ticks in the 'Yes' column indicates that the product status is probably static. A greater number of ticks in the 'No' column indicates that the product status is probably dynamic or potentially dynamic. Knowledge of this status can direct your emphasis in design, as described in Layer 4B of the design plan.

Now complete Questionnaire B Micro to see if your company status is the same as the product status. If there is a status mismatch, the company characteristics and disciplines you will need to emphasize are shown in Layer 4B of the design plan.

Support text L3.1 shows the advantage of using the questionnaire. Support text L3.2 shows another questionnaire (A2) which can be used to give a periodic check as to a product's status or an existing production item. Part 1, Section 4.4, shows the factors that make a product static or dynamic as determined from the research.

If you are unable to answer the questionnaire with confidence you have not completed the previous layers satisfactorily *Repeat Layer 2*. If your design proposal is *conceptually vulnerable* (the wrong concept, under threat from a better concept or treated as static when it is dynamic) *Return to Layer 1*. Remember:

1. It is possible for two conceptually different products to share the same market (e.g. cylinder and hover lawnmowers).
2. Circumstances change, and repeating these questionnaires in the future can warn you of a possible alteration in product status which may require a shift in your design emphasis, especially when an innovation appears.
3. You must compare like with like. A car does not become a dynamic product if the carburettor is changed to a fuel injection pump. It is the fuel feed system that is dynamic. You may therefore need a status check on the whole product or on some of its components or subsets.

If you are a large company in your industry it is in your interests to have a static product (ST L3.3).

Note: Questionnaire A Macro should be used as a check on an innovation to determine if it is a threat to your product or is likely to end the static plateau. If trying to break into a market with a new invention or technical advance, put yourself in the competitors' position and view your new product from their standpoint.

Third design review (ST I.2)

Layer 3 support text

L3.1 The advantages of using the questionnaires

The following five points demonstrate the advantage of using the status questionnaires in the design of products.

1. Having answered the questionnaires the user should know if the product is static, dynamic or about to change status and can therefore direct the design emphasis.
2. As one questionnaire refers to the product environment and the other to the way it is treated within a company it is possible to demonstrate if the company's way is 'in or out of step' with the environment/market.
3. The questionnaires can be answered, if the information is known, as a competing company would and therefore may be used as part of competition analysis.
4. If a new product concept is being developed (a new dynamic design), by using the potential advantages of the new dynamic design when answering questions 4 to 6 on the A Macro questionnaire it provides an indication as to whether the new dynamic design is capable of ending the existing static plateau hence whether it is worth pursuing the new concept or the extent to which that concept will need to be better than the current design in order to replace it.
5. The questionnaires appear to overcome the need to define at what point a technology change should be considered static or dynamic. For example, was the introduction of the plastic bucket a dynamic design when it is still functionally a bucket? The questionnaires may be used to compare a plastic bucket with a steel one or a bucket with an alternative form of water carrier. The questionnaires serve both types of design change provided that the criteria for comparison are established at the beginning.

L.3.2 Periodic check on product status

Questionnaire A2 Macro has been devised for this purpose. Ticks in the 'Yes' column indicate where the product status is more static. Those in the 'No' column show where the product status is potentially more dynamic.

Questionnaire A2 Macro should only be used if no innovation has been recently introduced that may threaten your market. Otherwise use Questionnaire A Macro.

L3.3 Company size and product status

It is often stated that small companies are more innovative than large ones. For example, a study by the US National Science Foundation in 1979 and reported in Parker (1980) showed that small US firms produced twenty-four times as many innovations per unit of expenditure as large ones, and many large corporations were seeking ways to motivate a more entrepreneurial behaviour. Few explanations are given as to why this should be. Rothwell (1985) states 'It appears that new firms, initially, are better adapted to exploit new techno-market regimes, breaking out from existing regimes within which established corporations for historical, cultural and institutional reasons might be rather strongly bound'. Peters and Waterman (1982) make the following observation:

> We strongly believe that the major reason big companies stop innovating is their dependence on big factories, smooth production flow, integrated operation, big-bet technology planning and rigid strategic direction setting. They forget how to learn and they quit tolerating mistakes. The company forgets what made it

	Yes (static)	No (dynamic)
Questionnaire A2 Macro: Periodic check on product status *Product name:*		
Since you last checked the product status:		
1. Have any new conformance standards been written for this product?		
2. Tick the 'Yes' column if your number of competitors has decreased, tick the 'No' column if it has increased. (If no change, leave blank.)		
3. If there has been any improvement in the following which makes the product more viable or attractive to customers tick the 'Yes' column. If the change makes the product less viable or attractive to customers tick the 'No' column. If no change, leave blank: (a) Economic climate (b) Legislation (c) Resources		
4. Has any company emerged recently to dominate this product market?		
Total		

successful in the first place, which is usually a culture that encouraged action, experiments, repeated tries.

In our research one firm said that large companies 'are slow on their feet' and another commented that large companies are 'slow to react to change'. One explanation for this could be that the organic design team structure found in small companies aids communication, but this is now possible in both small and large companies through design circles (see page 52).

The principle of product status helps to explain why small companies may be more innovative than large ones, by showing that it is in the interests of a large company to have a static product whereas it is more advantageous for a small company to have a dynamic one. Andrews (1975) has noted that 'It is in the interests of the small company to disturb the status quo in the market, whereas it is in the interests of a large company to preserve the status quo'.

With a static product, companies that can achieve the disciplines associated with increased process design and low-cost production (automation, rationalization, specialization, dedicated machinery, etc.) are most likely to succeed. These static disciplines require a large production volume and the volume which makes these disciplines viable is more likely, the longer a product remains static (Static 2). A larger company in an industry, or a company that has a large market share, is most likely to have the necessary production volume to achieve the economies of scale and make the investment required. Having made the investment, they are not only likely to be lower-cost producers than their competitors, they are also less likely to want to change the design which may render this process machinery less efficient or obsolete. Ehrlenspiel (1984) has drawn the same conclusions: 'High expenditure on production facilities can limit the designer through not allowing him to change the production method until the equipment has been paid off'. It is in the interest of large companies, therefore, to keep the design of the product static.

On the other hand, a small company, or one with a small market share, is unable to compete directly with a large company in low-cost production while the product is static. However, if the small company can make the product dynamic so that flexible production is required and dedicated manufacturing equipment is unsuitable or unviable it can diminish the advantage of economies of scale and can compete on more equal terms (if still at a disadvantage) with the larger companies in the industry. Innovation is expensive and time consuming, and companies will not innovate unless they have to, to prevent loss of market and eventual decline. It would appear that small companies have to innovate to compete now; otherwise they must seek a market niche in areas which do not interest the larger companies in the industry (e.g. specialist sports car companies). Large companies do not need to innovate with such urgency except to compete with other large companies in their industry. The fewer the product design changes and the more stable the production, the greater is their advantage. In short, a small company needs to keep a product dynamic, a large one needs to keep it static. Therefore by following their own interests small companies are more innovative than large ones.

An exception to this occurs in certain industries, such as drugs and aerospace, where innovation is led by large companies. This is because the high costs incurred during a long period of product development without any financial return for some years precludes all but the largest companies from being involved in innovation. Even so, the type of design undertaken in these industries is generally of a static nature. It could be argued that most aircraft and most drugs are static products.

Parker (1978) has provided two other advantages that a large company has over a small one in the field of innovation:

> The argument indicating the advantage of large companies in the Research and Development process tend to include a degree of market power as a beneficial influence. The large company should have a marked advantage in technical activity:
> (1) raising additional capital is cheaper;
> (2) market power should allow large firms to secure high returns and recoup expenses fast (p.67).

In spite of these exceptions, we believe that our previous comments may help to explain why small companies decline and fail as their product becomes static and they can no longer compete with large companies.

Up to this stage of design, the process has concentrated on consideration of the product. Layer 4A still concentrates on the product, but Layers 4B and 5 consider in more detail the company disciplines to support this product.

The design plan shows that a company usually starts to market and sell its product after it has completed Layer 4. Certain products are designed for mass production and for these types of products the company must first consider the disciplines associated with Layer 5. With other products, as the demand and production volume grows over a period of time, Layer 5 disciplines will become increasingly important, and these will be introduced as they become viable.

Layer 4A: Write the product design specification

The product design specification gives 'breadth' to the design and must be a full and thorough written document which covers all aspects of design. *It is the most important part of the design process* (ST L4A.1). It has been shown (Part 1, Section 3.3) that the cost of design rises geometrically as the design approaches production, and as mistakes made at the beginning of the design process are often carried

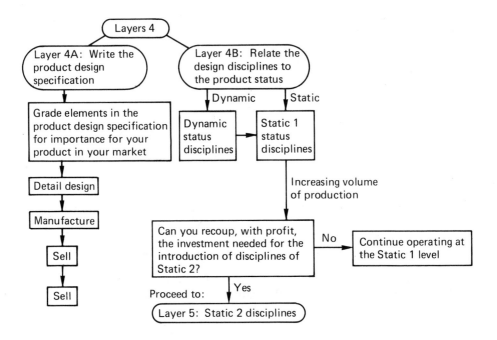

through into production it is essential that all aspects of the design are considered at this stage and written in the product design specification. All the elements of the PDS are shown in Figure 6.3 and described in ST L4A.2. Knowing your product status, some elements will be of more importance than others (ST L4A.3).

Part of the PDS represents the outcome of competition analysis which should include parametric analysis (ST L4A.4) which determines trends and product features. It is not necessary but advisable to carry out parametric analysis before this stage. The status questionnaire B Micro should also be used as a status check on a competitor. Put yourself in the position of a competitor and determine if it is operating at a static or a dynamic level. This can indicate if its future new products are likely to be static or dynamic designs and therefore aids your planning.

Also at this stage further marketing features should be investigated to determine market segmentation, market differentiation and national and/or international markets. The PDS can be written as an international specification with a national subsection if the product is to serve world markets.

It has been shown that it is possible to grade *some* of the elements in the PDS for importance (ST L4A.5) in a particular product serving a particular market. As design tends to be a compromise between the design elements, being able to state

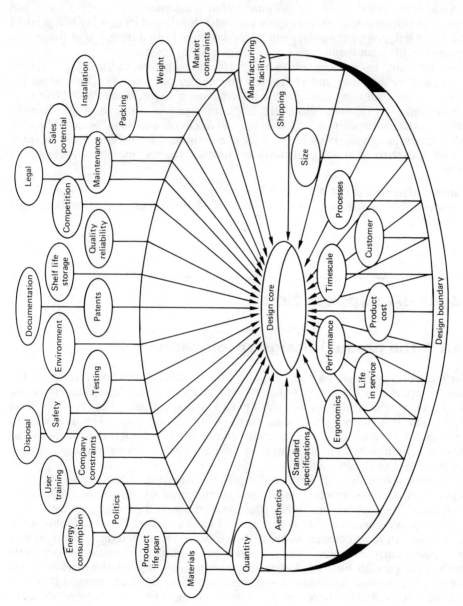

Figure 6.3 Elements of the product design specification

which are more or less important can aid the design emphasis. Whether the design is static or dynamic, product quality and reliability have been determined as the most important single elements. The grading may be considered as cost versus relative value to the customer or price/performance valuation.

Areas often overlooked are documentation (customer) (certainly a large and significant component of major capital projects), legal product liability and product disposal. Omission or misjudgement of the last two, both during and at the end of a product's life, can mean high economic and social costs.

The emerging instructions are to be interpreted by people in the design circle as to be used in directing and controlling the design process. As a first stage for gathering and compiling much of the information in the PDS see Wall (1986).

Although the PDS must utilize the latest information available, it may have to include some assumptions which later may be discovered to be incorrect. The PDS must be continually updated in the light of improved information. These changes should be confirmed at design reviews and justified to other members of the design circle.

Fourth design review (ST I.2)
Following the compilation of the PDS, product concepts are considered and evaluated.

Layer 4A support text

L4A.1 The product design specification

Corfield (1979) has given a high priority to the product design specification in the NEDO report and Lock (1968) has found irrelevance and diversification in the design of products caused by substandard specifications. The Institution of Production Engineers (1984) went further, observing that 'The majority of companies do not compile and therefore do not work to formal specifications and thus by definition are not in control of their product development and ergo are not in control of their business'.

In our research one of the most surprising discoveries (and one of the most depressing) was the woeful inadequacy of the product design specification in companies. The authors anticipated that companies would generally have prepared a fairly complete written PDS before embarking on design. This was found not to be the case. In most companies the PDS was brief, incomplete and based on very little and poorly organized market research. Companies appear to drift into product design with little market research or no idea of what the market needs. Conversely, the most successful companies were those that had the most thorough and the longest PDS. There are 35 elements in the PDS, and each needs to be considered. Not all may be important with any particular product but the design team will not know if an element is so until it has, at least, been considered.

Apart from the immediate advantage of a greater likelihood of product success there is a longer-term advantage for writing a full PDS as subsequent product model changes become more a matter of 'topping up' on the information already compiled with the addition of latest market trends, changes in technology or new competition, etc. that have occurred since the original PDS was written. In this total design process certain elements are considered at a stage earlier than compilation of the PDS to determine if it is advisable to abandon the project before a full specification is compiled. If the design still appears viable these elements will be included in the PDS.

The PDS is sometimes known as 'Target Specification', 'Design Brief', 'Primary Specification' or 'Statement of Requirements'. None of these names imply the importance of completeness necessary in the document.

L4A.2 The contents of the product design specification

A PDS contains all the facts relating to the product outcome. It should try to avoid 'leading' the design and predicting this outcome, but nevertheless it should also contain the realistic constraints to be imposed upon the design by either the company or the market. In terms of modern, competitive practice, the starting point for any design activity must be market research, followed by competition analysis, literature searching, patent extracting, etc., from which a comprehensive PDS must be prepared. Products based upon a 'blank sheet of paper' design, singleton ideas (Eurekas), unless extremely fortunate and lucky, are unlikely to compete with, say, Japanese products. To be successful one has to be systematic and thorough, paying meticulous attention to detail from the beginning to the end of the total design activity. The PDS is the fundamental control mechanism which helps success to be achieved.

The specification is the basic reference source – it is the main control for the whole of the product design activity. It should be borne in mind that the PDS is evolutionary and that it is a dynamic not a static document. A PDS evolves and changes with the emergence of the design; if, during the design of a particular artefact there is a good reason for changing the basic PDS, then change it.

The PDS, while recognized as being evolutionary, must be underwritten by all the sectors of a business. It must not remain the responsibility of one area. All areas must contribute to this evolution, especially at the beginning since unsound starts are difficult to recover from later. The PDS must be a written document which, upon completion of the design, matches the product itself and forms the natural basis for the specification of the product as designed.

The PDS must be made comprehensive and written in terms understandable by all departments of a business. All businesses are primarily about products for markets; if this primary criterion is not continually satisfied, profits either never materialize or are, at best, not maintained.

Many organizations are now requesting academic institutions and industry to teach and practice design in a comprehensive manner. While they are not considered to be sufficiently explicit, their collective pronouncements all contain some of the elements of what should be the basis of a comprehensive PDS, albeit in an unstructured way. Also, they do add weight to the arguments so far and in the following section.

The headings of a PDS represent the primary 'elements' to bring about the formulation of a comprehensive specification. In using them, the reader will find that, progressively, they start to overlap and integrate. As this happens, there will be a great tendency to 'cut and run', which is to be avoided at all costs, since submission to it leads to a less than adequate PDS. Such product design specifications are often incomplete and therefore inadequate.

The preparation of a PDS is a discipline in itself, and, as noted above, consists of 35 primary elements which must be considered prior to the commencement or as part of a design. The PDS forms the main design control, and the collective elements represent the design boundary. Incidentally, they also remove the necessity for a preponderance of 'gut feeling', which still looms large in UK product designs and which is not good enough to meet competition from Japan.

Performance

The performance demanded or likely to be demanded from a product should be fully defined: how fast, how slow, how often, continuously or discontinuously, loadings likely, electrical, hydraulic or pneumatic, tolerance of speed, rate of working, etc. Remember that usually the more complex the product, the more likelihood there is of ambiguities and conflict in the performance figure specified.

Is the performance demanded attainable economically? A common failing in specifying performance is to ask for the ultimate rather than that which is obtainable. It is easy to tighten up a performance specification to such an extent that if one was designed to meet that performance the customer would not be willing or able to afford it – even if the company could make it in the first place. Sales departments and clients never cease to be surprised that, from their specification, such an expensive product emerges.

While the practice of overspecifying (belt and braces) sometimes occurs in mass production industries, it is more likely with specialist equipment, particularly in the large, one-off field, where clients do not really know the level of performance needed for their requirements. Beware, therefore, of overspecification of performance and also remember that performance is but one component of the PDS.

Environment

Any product is subject to a number of environments during both its manufacture and usage, particularly between its primary manufacture (i.e. piece parts (components), assembly and test, packaging, transportation and storage) and its intended use. Environment is thus one significant primary element which needs analysis and emphasis in a PDS and gives rise to one of the most significant interactions between PDS elements. The following aspects should always be considered:

Temperature range
Pressure range (altitude)
Humidity
Shock loading (gravity forces)
Dirty or dusty – how dirty? How clean?
Corrosion from fluids – type of fluid or chemical
Noise levels
Insects
Vibration
Type of labour or persons who will use the equipment – likely degree of abuse?
Any unforeseen hazards?

under the five categories of:

Factory floor
Packaged
Storage
Transportation
Use

In many instances the performance requirements are also closely related to the environment and may be called upon to vary with it.

Life in service (performance)

Should service life be short or long, and on what criteria? Against which part of the PDS is (or should) the product life be assessed? One year on full performance, 24 hours a day, 7 days a week? This must be settled before starting a design.

Maintenance

Is regular maintenance available or desirable? Will designing for maintenance-free operation prejudice the design to such an extent that the product will become too expensive to buy in the first place? Does the company, or indeed the market into which the product will ultimately go, have a definitive maintenance policy? Is the market used to maintaining equipment once it is purchased? The following points are relevant:

Specify ease of access to the parts likely to require maintenance. It is no good calling for regular maintenance if it takes ten days to reach the part! What is the maintenance and spares philosophy of the company and market? Spares holdings, availability, and for how long? The likely need and desirability of special tools for maintenance.

Target product cost

Target product costs should be established from the outset and checked against existing or similar products. It can be said with certainty that almost all target costs are on the low side and in many cases unattainable within the terms of the PDS.

Care should be taken at this stage to ascertain whether the target cost is compatible with competitors' products and, *most importantly*, with the manufacturing facility available to make the product. Cost patterns should be established and studied in detail before setting the target cost.

If a whole-life costing attitude is being adopted by the company, then this should be considered, with particular reference to maintenance trade-off and downtime.

Competition

A thorough analysis of the competition must be carried out, including a comprehensive patents and literature search relating not only to the proposed product area but also to analogous areas. These must be analysed. The nature and extent of existing and likely competition is probably the most important aspect of a PDS, at least from a comparative viewpoint. If, for example the evolving specification shows serious mismatches or deficiencies when compared with what already exists, then the reasons for such departures must be fully understood. Therefore it is essential that a full parametric analysis be carried out. Remember, it is very easy to re-invent an inferior teapot!

Typical magnitudes of such searches for products are:

Research papers	300–600
Patents	10–100
Competitive, comparable and analogous products	2–80
Parametric graphs	5–75

Remember that, to date, very few competitors do this thoroughly or systematically.

Shipping

It is necessary to determine how the product is to be delivered: by land, sea or air; home or overseas; type and size of truck; pallet container (ISO); type of aircraft used for the product under consideration. It is not unknown for equipment not to be able to pass through cargo hatches of aircraft or ships or to be expensive in terms of shipping volume. This can affect the subassembly breakdown of the product. Lifting capability and provision of lifting points must be ensured. A product may be competitive in the UK but by the time it is shipped overseas it may have become too expensive.

Packing

According to the type of product being designed, some form of packaging for transport, storage, etc. may be necessary. The cost of packing will add to product cost and volume. Can the packing withstand environmental effects such as corrosion, shock-loading, etc? What are these? (See Environment.)

Quantity

Likely numbers of or size of run will affect all aspects of a product design. A one-off will probably require very little tooling; moderate numbers may require cheap temporary tooling, while large numbers off may require permanent, expensive tooling. This has a considerable effect on the supportive investment required and the plant already existing in-house.

Manufacturing facility

Are you designing to fill an existing plant or is the plant and machinery involved a constraint to the design of our product? What are the plans for new plant and machinery? It is no good designing for a particular process route only to find a new one in existence by the time the production phase is reached.

Degree of correlation and interaction between product and process design depends to a large degree on product status. Make-in or buy-out policy; is the product to be constrained or restricted to techniques with which the company is familiar and has experience? Is the proposed flexible manufacturing system the ultimate in inflexibility? Do you need to concentrate more on a process design?

Size

Is there any restriction on the size of the product? Sizes should be specified initially. So many designs grow like Topsy – the result being that the product will not fit in the space provided or deemed acceptable. Is access for cleaning and maintenance likely to be difficult? Are shape constraints (e.g. length × breadth × height) important? Your innovative Sony Walkman replacement 1 metre long would not impress customers!

Weight

For a given technology, weight is frequently directly related to cost. Allied to its size, weight is important when handling the product on the shopfloor during manufacture, in transit, during installation or in the user situation.

Aesthetics, appearance and finish

The appearance of a product is difficult to specify and therefore, in many instances, is left to the design team: the complaints come afterwards. Colour, shape, form and texture of finish should always be considered from the outset. Advice and opinion should always be sought either from within the company or without.

Sales, marketing, production and others will always criticize a design once it exists. Efforts should be made to obtain these opinions before the design commences. Every person is a design critic, accomplished or otherwise. So often the final appearance of a product 'just happens', and then strenuous efforts are made to make it look better, which usually prejudices the design in all aspects. Never forget, whatever the product, the customers *see* it first before they buy it. The physical performance comes later, *the visual always first.*

Materials

The choice of materials for a particular product design is invariably left to the designer. Usually this is not a bad thing. However, if special materials are necessary they should be specified, preferably by quoting the appropriate standard. The converse is also true. If it is known that certain materials must not be used they should also be specified (e.g. toxic materials in consumer products, aluminium or its alloys on exposed surfaces for underground coal-mining equipment).

Product life span

Some indication of the life of a product as a marketable entity should be sought. Is it likely to remain in production for 2 years or 20 years? The answers here can affect the design approach and interact with the market and competition, tooling policy, investment in manufacturing, etc.

Standards and specifications

Is the product to be designed to current international and/or British Standards? If so, then these should be specified and copies obtained. Cross correlation of such standards should be carried out prior to the commencement of design. Remember that it is difficult, costly, time consuming and inefficient to attempt retrospective matching of designs already finalized to other standards.

Ergonomics

All products have, to some degree, a man–machine interface. It is therefore necessary to clarify the likely nature of the interaction of the product with man. What height, reach, forces and operating torques are acceptable? Postures, lighting, etc. should also be considered. Is the product, because of its appearance, likely to be mistakenly used in some mode other than that for which it was intended? Is it to be operated in a way similar to a competitor's product, even if the basic specifications are different?

Customer

Who is the customer? Usually one thinks only of the ultimate user, the person who, for example, rides the bicycle or listens to the radio. It is essential to define just who the customer is and to establish his or her requirements. As products progress through the manufacturing chain, they will have varying customers with differing needs.

For its effective implementation, quality function deployment relies heavily on the 'voice of the customer'. The customer's voice manifests itself in sets of constraints which, for reliability and accuracy, depend very much on the status of the product. Static products will have well developed and sophisticated constraints, dynamic ones less so.

The degree of difficulty in obtaining this input varies considerably, from the large one-off turnkey type of project, where designers will interface directly with the customer, to the mass-produced one, where traditionally they will not. This must change, and even for mass-produced products, to be successful design teams must have access to customers.

Quality and reliability

Levels of quality and reliability necessary to ensure product success and acceptability in a particular market are a cause of increasing concern. They are the most difficult aspects to quantify in absolute terms, although statistical data from company product precedents are helpful here. In electronics, mean time before failure (MTBF) and mean time to repair (MTTR) are familiar expressions, although it must be remembered that, in comparison with mechanical, hydraulic, pneumatic and even electrical components, electronic products have a relatively controlled, sheltered life. Nonetheless, some quantitative expression must be made in respect of quality and reliability at the specification stage. Here reference should be made to:

- BS 5750, *Quality systems* (5 parts), Part 4: 1981.
- Guide to Use of BS 5750, Part 1: *Specification for design, manufacture and installation*.
- BS 5760: *Reliability of systems and equipment and components* (3 parts).
- The work of Dr Genichi Taguchi on quality loss function, parameter design and the design of experiments.

A company must ensure adequate feedback of failure from whatever the source, for analysis by the design team.

Shelf life (storage)

A factor often overlooked in specifications is that of a 'shelf life' (as applied to units) or storage on site (as applied to complete plant). In respect of units, shelf life must be specified at the outset and the means to combat decay considered (see Environment). Otherwise rusty gearboxes, perished rubber components, seized bearings, defective electronics, defective linings, corrosion and general decay may occur.

The designer of a complex plant should also be aware of these problems since equipment designed on the assumption of immediate installation and commissioning may lie on-site for months without adequate protection and storage.

Processes

In-house process specifications, as opposed to manufacturing techniques, are vitally important. If special processes are to be used during manufacture they should be defined (e.g. plating or wiring specifications, or, alternatively, the relevant British or International Standards).

Timescales

Lead times allowed for design are frequently inadequate, but they determine the timescale for the whole project up to manufacture and product launch. Design time must ensure that the product is designed effectively and efficiently – in other words, professionally. Lack of adequate time spent at the beginning of a design project will be made up for later to other people's timescales when we have defective products, market mismatches, overwhelming competition, etc. There is no alternative to adequate design time.

Testing

Most products require some form of testing after manufacture, either in the factory, on-site or both. Products for the consumer or engineering markets usually require a factory test to verify their quality and compliance with the product design specification. Curiously, this usually relates to the performance aspects which, although essential, represent a narrow view of the whole question of product evolution.

Do we sample test one in ten or one in a hundred? Do we need a new test facility? How can we be sure that the product is designed to have rapid engagement with and detachment from the test rig? Data and product history, etc. must be known and an *ab-initio* test specification should be written at this stage. After the design is completed is too late (see Quality and reliability).

Process plants and projects of this nature usually have acceptance and witness tests called for in addition to factory tests. As with all testing, these require careful planning and execution in order not only to ensure compliance with the PDS but also to limit cost.

Safety

Safety aspects of the proposed design and its place in the market must be considered. Indeed, there may be legislation and standards covering these, such as the Health and Safety at Work Acts, EEC directives on product liability and specifications relevant to particular product areas (e.g. BS 5724: Safety Requirements on Hospital Medical Electrical Equipment).

Labelling should give adequate warnings. Likely degrees of abuse, whether obvious or not, should also be considered as well as misrepresentation of the equipment's function. Definitive operating instructions must be prepared. The safety aspect of the proposed design in its environment must be considered (e.g. finger traps, misuse (see Ergonomics), abuse, toxic finishes, inflammable materials, corrosion leading to structural decay and an ultimate hazard to people). Does the paint contain lead? Are there sharp edges and corners, proximity of exposed contacts during maintenance? The list is almost endless.

Legal

The legal aspects of product design have been highlighted as a primary trigger additional to general safety aspects that apply to all products (e.g. the Health and Safety at Work Acts and product liability legislation, both EEC and North American).

Abbott (1980) states that 'probably design is responsible for more product failures than anything else', and then attaches great importance to the PDS. It is the authors' view that, in any case relating to product failure causing financial loss, injury or even death it will pay to have a thoroughly documented PDS, since lawyers may have recourse to all documentation pertaining to a product's evolution. In our terms it will be necessary to distinguish between the following:

● *Defect of specification (PDS).* Should it have been foreseen at the outset that the product would be misused or abused or should *not* have embodied a certain feature (say)?
● *Defect of engineering.* The PDS had been perfect but something had broken due to bad engineering.
● *Defect of manufacture.* The PDS had been perfect, the engineering *design* (in conventional terms) was also perfect, but defective material had been used or machined to a wrong tolerance.

The legal aspects of the PDS are thus becoming very important.

Company constraints

The constraints of current company practice should be highlighted and discussed. Is the company constrained by its previous products? If so, it is important to know this at the specification stage. Possible manufacturing constraints, financial and investment restrictions and staff attitudes are very relevant. Are there adequate in-house facilities for research, design, development, testing, etc. – including quality of personnel?

Market constraints

Feedback from the marketplace should be considered. It is no use incorporating a certain firm's engines into equipment for some Middle East countries if those countries will not accept them. Local conditions (particularly overseas) and full knowledge of the market, its ambience and customers must be fed into the PDS at the beginning.

Patents, literature and product data

All areas of potentially useful information should be investigated and duplication of existing patents should be known as soon as possible. It is pointless designing something for sale in ignorance of someone else's patent.

Political and social implications

The likely effect of the product on the political and social structures of the market or country for which it is to be designed and manufactured should be considered (e.g. the effect of consumer movements, the stability of the market, product features to avoid which can create social unrest, etc.).

Installation

Many products must interface with other products or be assembled into larger ones (e.g. buildings). Installation, therefore, must be considered in the PDS. This will include fixing holes and lugs, access and volume available for the product, system and power compatibility, etc.

Energy consumption

This takes two forms, the energy usage of the product (e.g. battery life in the design of a radio) and that used in manufacture (e.g. the tonnage of a press needed to form a component). The former is more important in most designs, but the latter will be more relevant in mass-produced products and thus to consumer perceptions.

User training

User training may need to be given especially with dynamic products, new products or those where the operator needs to be skilled. This should be considered in the PDS and arrangements made for the preparation of user manuals and training schemes.

Sales potential

Clearly, there is little purpose in pursuing a design if the sales potential is small. However, the sales potential also determines how the product is made and marketed. Identify the sales potential in the PDS and relate it to other elements.

Documentation

Product documentation is always important in terms of instructions to the user, maintainer, etc. Even with consumer products, it is an important and vital task that must not be shirked (see Safety and Legal). With large turnkey projects (e.g. power stations) the associated documentation can become a substantial part of the overall design task. It also occupies a more important position in relation to dynamic rather than static products, as customer familiarity with the latter will be much greater than with the former.

Disposal

Disposal has been included as a primary element as the effects of man's design of products increasingly impinges on our environment. With many products, services or spare parts must be provided after ownership has passed to the customer. Also, if the product contains hazardous or toxic parts (or indeed parts worth reclaiming) these should be considered at the PDS stage. Similarly, the demolition of buildings or oil platforms must be included in an architect's or engineer's PDS. This is covered more fully in ST L4A6.

While the above represent the primary elements enabling the preparation of a PDS, we must never forget that a specification will and should be subject to amendment and alteration with the passage of time and is, therefore, evolutionary. Upon completion of a design, the specification may be suitably enlarged with detail and, almost by definition, will provide the basic material for handbooks, sales and technical literature. It becomes the specification of the product itself rather than that for its design. Therefore it provides the basis for the user or producer to make decisions in a comprehensive way.

Remember, there are no alternatives to a meticulous and thorough approach to PDS preparation in a competitive world. The PDS is defined as that which sets out in detail the requirements to be met to achieve a successful product or process. When the product has been designed, it is itself specified by the drawings, documentation, etc. which describe the product in great depth. This is known as the specification of the product – *the product specification.* Try to avoid the use of loose semantics where one description may be confused with another.

Note that many of the elements relate to or depend on other elements (e.g. sales potential/quantity/processes/materials). As the first draft of the PDS is written, review its content with these various relationships in mind.

The PDS document

Guidelines for preparation:

1. Remember that the PDS is a control document; it represents the specification of what you are trying to achieve – not of the achievement itself.
2. The PDS is a user document – for use by you and others. It should therefore be written succinctly and clearly.
3. Never write a PDS in essay form. Use short definitive statements under the headings provided above. It is useful in practice to allow space for amendment and additions. Therefore do not crowd the page: two to four headings per page are usually adequate.

4. From the beginning, try to be quantitative in each area (e.g. weight, size, cost, temperature, etc.). If you do not know, or are in doubt, estimate a figure.
5. Since a PDS is always unique in a new design situation (i.e. dynamic), the relationship between the elements always varies. It is recommended that in preparing a PDS you also vary your starting point (e.g. you may start one PDS with Performance and another with Environment or Politics). Varying the starting point will aid the acquisition of the flexibility of thinking required to prepare good PDSs.
6. Always date the document and put an issue number on it (i.e. 1-1-89 Issue 1, 2-7-89 Issue 2).
7. Clearly document amendments.

L4A.3 Product status in relation to the product design specification

Product status in no way diminishes the importance of the product design specification in its entirety. However, knowing whether a product is static or dynamic enables certain elements in the product design specification to be highlighted, so some of them become relatively more important and others less so.

Dynamic product
Relatively more important than in a static product design. Increased activity related to:

Product	Company
Design protection (e.g. patents)	In-house training
Market definition	Customer training
Customer definition	Niche marketing (skimming)
Seeking new concepts	Flexible production
Innovation	Subcontract manufacture
Advanced technical features	Open management

Static product
Relatively more important than in a dynamic product. Increased activity related to:

Product	Company
Aesthetics	Process design
Ergonomics	Purchasing
Incremental improvements	Competition analysis
Product cost reduction	Parametric analysis
Energy use in product	Energy use on production
Imitation	Rationalization
Value analysis	Mass marketing
Rationalization	Automation
Conformance standards	Large producer
CAD	
Using experience in design	

The above can be used in competition analysis to identify how the competitors are operating.

L4A.4 Parametric analysis

Parametric analysis is an inexpensive form of desk research which has proved to be a powerful tool for both marketing and design. It is used both to identify a product's place in the market in relation to the competition and also to gain insight into the make-up and interrelationships between the parameters inherent in the products under consideration. It should always be included as an essential part of the information fed into the PDS. This means analysis of competing products from a consideration, at least initially, of published catalogue data. Such an analysis is primarily concerned with the seeking out of relationships between parameters for the particular product area under consideration. This, by definition, means cross plotting such parameters to find the existence of relationships between them. In a realistic situation, cross plots of large amounts of data are made – usually by a computer program. To be of full value, in practice one produces literally hundreds of parameter cross plots. Although, in most instances, probably half of these show no relationship, the other half may show strong relationships which, almost invariably, were previously unknown.

A word of warning: in order to carry out a comprehensive analysis it is essential that the participants be happy, willing and able to do the many cross plots necessary without, in the *first instance*, being able to deduce the reason for so doing. In other words, the particular cross plot may, prior to carrying it out, appear to be illogical.

This illogicality causes problems for many engineers. If they cannot see the logic of a situation then they cannot or will not start work, and will dismiss the exercise as trivial. This is not to say that parameters having traditional, logical relationships should not be plotted. Nevertheless, usually the greatest amount of useful information stems from apparently illogical plots. In such cases, having 'seen' the relationships established, the logic has been retrofitted. Without the visual parametric painting, the discovery of the relationship would be unlikely.

So what are the rules and guidelines for parametric analysis?

1. Assemble as much information as possible on one's own and competitors' products.
2. Establish a label for both company and model number and, if required, one to identify significant conceptual difference (i.e. specification achieved by using a different approach).
3. Use colour to aid the distinctions of 2.
4. Cross plot the data in graphical form and look for patterns and relationships between parameters – the parametric painting.
5. Ensure that the data being used relate to comparable products at the same generic level (i.e. cars cannot meaningfully be compared with sewing machines except at the subsystem or component level (e.g. spindles).
6. Always start with logical relationships – these are usually covered very quickly and usually, relative to the whole, are very few.
7. Do not try to be clever. Use the data in their raw state and then, having gained a greater understanding from the initial plots, useful combined parameters may emerge.
8. Look for and try to establish strong patterns, the existence of which is confirmed by retrofitting the logic. No apparent logic, no valid retrofit is usually the case.

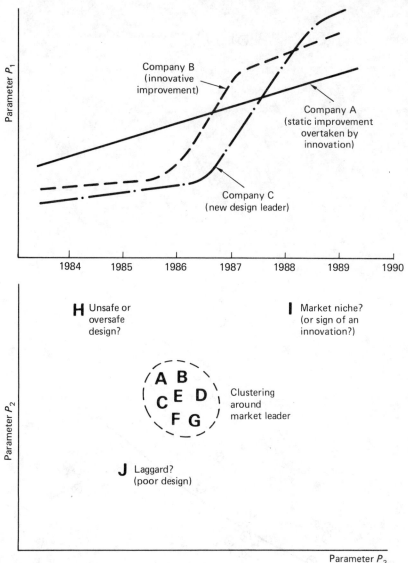

Figure 6.4 Typical parametric plots

9. Place the promising plots side by side on a wall or board – preferably very large – and compare one with another. It is essential they be viewed collectively since this usually establishes further missing logic and gives rise to explanations which are then seen to be obvious. Grouping of plots incorporating the same parameters is always useful and revealing.
10. Look for exceptions to strong patterns; these are usually due to:
    (a) A wrong plot.
    (b) The particular model is exceptional (why?).
    (c) The model is not to the same generic base.

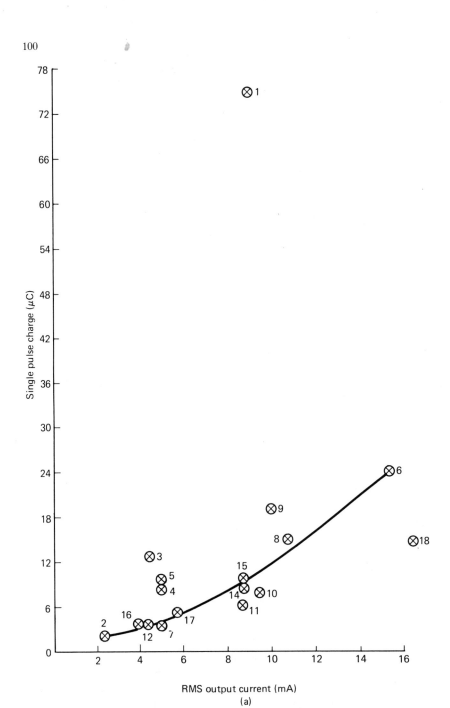

Figure 6.5 Features analysis for pain relief devices: (a) single pulse charge versus RMS output current; (b) price/kg versus weight. (Courtesy NPM International)

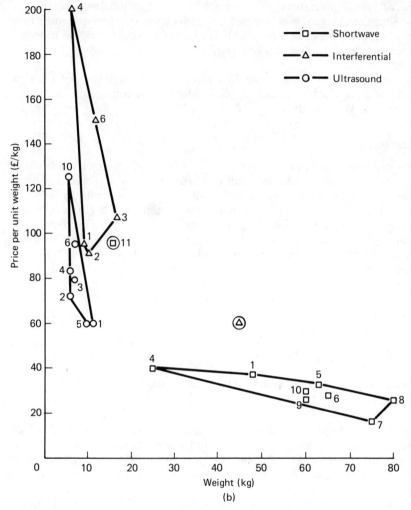

Figure 6.5 *continued*

11. Always draw conclusions from the plots: if relationships have been established, retain them; if not, they should be discarded.
12. Correlate the findings with traditional market research data.
13. Use the knowledge gained as an input into the PDS.

In a typical case, several hundred plots will be made. From these, twenty to fifty will be found to be useful and one or two highly significant, and all, in the main, not known previously, even to experts in the field (Figure 6.4). In one instance we identified a potentially dangerous design which was initially observed as being at the 'risky' extreme of the parametric plot and well away from the other manufacturers. The company was informed and took the appropriate action to rectify a situation of which it was completely unaware. Clustering of plots around a market leader is revealing in that it occurs because of rationalization, though using similar suppliers (e.g. diesel engines for generating equipment) and often because of imitation. This can be an indication of a static product or 'me tooism'. Products appearing at the fringes of a plot may be indicative of a company seeking a market niche.

Parametric analysis is also useful at the subsystem or component level of a design (e.g. for assessing a group of potential suppliers who are providing components to be incorporated into your products).

Features analysis

Another powerful tool is that of features analysis (Figure 6.5), in which the features of product specification can be plotted against a base of time (e.g. product weight, size of engine, power output, cost, number of integrated circuits or even of producers). Continuously updated, this will demonstrate which companies are leading, lagging or changing their designs, in which areas the greatest changes are occurring, and if the market is growing or contracting. It may also reveal in which area particular companies are concentrating their design effort.

Also radical changes in performance may indicate those aspects of a design that may have become dynamic and require further investigation. Lack of change in performance over a period of time may indicate that a design format is hardening or even becoming completely static. A declining number of manufacturers may also suggest that the design is becoming static or at least is being treated as such.

L4A.5 Grading the elements of the product design specification

The Feilden Report (1963) stressed the importance of 'non-price' factors, which include reliability, appearance, ease of use and maintenance, comfort, safety, prompt delivery and performance. In this section an attempt is made to determine the relative importance of these, which are mostly elements in the product design specification.

Rothwell and Gardiner (1984) looked at the important factors in machinery purchasing decisions of 105 British farmers (mixed farms) (Table 6.1). These were

Table 6.1 Ranking of factors in farm machinery purchase (from Rothwell and Gardiner, 1984)

Factor	Average	Ranking
Reliability in use	1	NP (II)
Overall technical quality	2	NP (II)
Speed of spares supply	3	NP (I)
Work capacity/speed	4	NP (II)
Ease of maintenance	5	NP (II)
Ease of use	6	NP (II)
Quality of after-sales service	7	NP (I)
Sales price	8	P
Ability to meet quoted delivery	9	NP (I)
Choice offered by local agents	10	NP (I)

Table 6.2 Overall rating of product attributes: analysis of West German and UK users (1 = very important, 9 = not important) (from Parkinson, 1981)

Product attribute	1	3	5	7	9	
Accuracy	76	23	0.8	0	0	%
Reliability	91	9	0	0	0	
Flexibility	33	39	23	4	0	
Price	33	37	25	5	0	
Delivery	33	40	24	3	0	
Power	36	28	25	9	1	
Maximum size of workpiece	23	40	24	7	5	
Rigidity	48	36	14	1	1	
Standardization of parts	30	36	23	10	2	
Technical sophistication	36	26	26	10	3	
Speed of operation	53	29	16	2	1	

Table 6.3 Ranking of their own products' features by manufacturers of two types of product

Factor (construction vehicles)	Ranking	Factor (suspension components)	Ranking
Quality and reliability	= 1	Reliability	1
Safety	= 1	Strength	2
Maintainability	= 3	Advanced technical features	3
Ease of use (ergonomics)	= 3	Maintainability	4
Strength	5	Low price	= 5
Long working life	6	Ease of use (ergonomics)	= 5
Low price	7	Finish	7
Appearance	= 8	Appearance	8
Fast delivery	= 8	Colour	9
Finish	10		
Advanced technical features	11		
Conforming to standards	12		
Small size and weight	13		
Colour	14		
Low energy use	15		
Long shelf life	16		

listed and signified as price (P) and non-price (NP), factors NP (I) being convenience and NP (II) quality.

In another study by Parkinson (1981) comparing British and West German machine tool manufacturers the question was asked: 'How important do you believe the following factors are when you are considering the purchase of a new machine tool of relatively standard design?' The results were as shown in Table 6.2.

In our research we sought from the manufacturer a ranking of the relative features they considered important for their product in their market. They were asked to rank the features between 'very important' and 'very unimportant' in five steps. 'Very important' was given two marks, reducing by one mark at each step to −2 for 'very unimportant'. The results are shown in Table 6.3. The total number of factors questioned is shown; the list of factors for suspension components was much shorter than that for construction vehicles (Figure 6.6).

By extracting the product attributes from the studies by Rothwell and Gardiner (R&G) and Parkinson (P) that can be compared with our research, and then putting them in order of importance, the results in Table 6.4 are obtained. Few

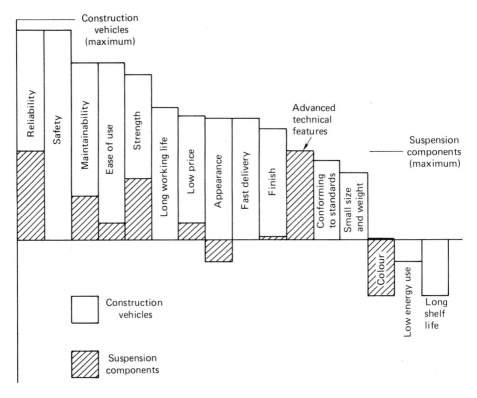

Figure 6.6

Table 6.4 Overview of the three studies

Factor	Ranking			
	P (1981)	R&G (1984)	Suspension components	Construction vehicles
Reliability	1	1	1	1
Overall technical quality/power/rigidity/strength	4	2	2	4
Speed of spares supply/fast delivery	3	3	–	6
Ease of maintenance/standardisation of parts	5	4	4	=2
Ease of use	–	5	6	=2
Sales price	2	6	5	5
Advanced technical features/technical sophistication	6	–	3	7

factors appear in both tables, and some have been considered as the same without being exactly so (e.g. 'speed of delivery' = 'speed of spares supply', 'strength' = 'overall technical quality').

Of the six features directly comparable, 'reliability' is shown to be most important in all three cases. 'Sales price' appears to be relatively unimportant, as does 'ease of use'. It must be remembered, though, that these six factors are probably more important than many others that have not been listed. For example, 'colour' and 'long shelf life' are of significantly less importance than 'low price'.

This demonstrates the overall importance of product reliability in product design and shows why it should be considered early in the product design process. Reliability has been much quoted as one of the reasons for the success of Japanese design.

Apart from grading the elements of the specification for importance, as described, certain elements are clearly more (or less) important, depending on the type of product being designed. If the product cannot easily be seen *in situ*, then colour and appearance are of less importance. Similarly, a low sound volume is an advantage in a car but a disadvantage in a radio, so performance features must be viewed in relation to the product under review.

L4A.6 Product disposal

With many products it is not possible to 'forget' about them after they have been sold to customers. Spare parts and servicing is often necessary and therefore spares must be made available, often for many years after the product has been manufactured, and personnel must be instructed in servicing an item which no longer may be on sale. This requires a decision on how long spare parts will be available and at what rate they will be used. This is because stockholding of these spare parts will be required often after the parts have ceased to be produced and these parts may degrade over time.

Warehouse space used in holding these stocks can be wasted space and give a poor return on the capital tied up in it and the stock. The great saving claimed by reducing warehousing in one aspect of JIT (ST L5.7) is an indication of the possible cost of storing these spare parts for many years, most of which must come out of the return made from the original product. This also helps to explain the high cost charged for many spare parts.

The need to store and supply spare parts is a burden that should be considered in the original design. It may warrant the need to consider designing a disposable product that might have a slightly higher original manufactured cost but overcomes the necessity of providing spare parts. This, in turn, puts a greater emphasis on reliability so that the product lasts for an acceptable length of time and gives a performance that customers will accept knowing that they will be unable to extend the life of the product if any part is broken or worn out.

Certain products may include components or materials that the company may wish to reclaim or re-use. For example, X-ray photographic plates contain an amount of silver, and this can be reclaimed. A lead/acid battery also contains re-usable materials, as do many other products. The cost of reclaiming must be considered and also it may create a need for the design of a process or machine to assist in this retrieval.

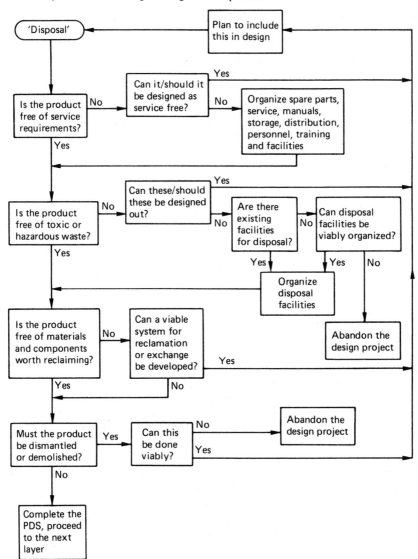

Figure 6.7 Flow diagram for product disposal

This should be considered at the PDS and product detailing stage. Similarly, the company may wish to reclaim entire units from customers for re-use, such as exchange alternators and starter motors in the car industry. This will involve an infrastructure to enable customers to bring in their old parts and exchange them for new or serviced parts. These returned parts will be returned to the factory and made serviceable. If this format is to be adopted the product must be designed so that its component parts can be easily disassembled for re-use, a decision that should be taken at the PDS and detailing stage (Figure 6.7).

When they have finished their useful life some products cannot easily be disposed of. Nothing has brought this so sharply into focus than the current problems of closing the now-outdated Magnox nuclear reactors that came into service in the early 1960s. Insufficient consideration was given in the original design as to how these power stations could be 'switched off' after their relatively short design life of 20 years (later extended to 30 years). Only now are the full cost and difficulties being appreciated, and the cost of disposal in this case will exceed the original build cost (in today's money). Thus the cost of the power that was generated was significantly less profitable than was realized at the time.

The case of atomic power stations is an extreme example, but many products include toxic or hazardous materials that cannot always be left to the customer to dispose of in the assumption that it will be done wisely. The cost of reclaiming these hazardous materials is likely to be relatively high and often difficult. Then there is the problem of finding a suitable place for safe disposal. It may be possible to avoid using such substances in the design and perhaps these can be substituted by other, more expensive, materials which can avoid the disposal problem. This is becoming an increasingly contentious and legislated area. The use of toxic materials should be considered at the PDS and detailing stage of design.

In time, all buildings will require dismantling and they can impose extensive costs that must be planned before the building is erected. For example, demolition of a high-rise building typically costs in excess of £1 million. The law demands that oil platforms are demolished to within 2 metres of the seabed and the cost of this has been estimated at up to £80 million per platform.

An important aspect of design is to identify how long the product should last. Should obsolescence be designed in? Cars should last for a period comparable with competitors' models to avoid, for example, having a poor reputation for corrosion. On the other hand, reducing the effects of corrosion can usually only be achieved with an increase in cost of manufacture and penalties in terms of performance due to the additional weight. This should be considered at the PDS stage. How long should the product last to be competitive but cost effective? This applies to most other consumer durables as well as foods, which should have a shelf life comparable to those of competitors' products.

Built-in obsolescence can be a useful attribute for many products that may have a short practical life. For example, biodegradable plastic may be an ecologically more acceptable material for food packaging than the non-biogradable type. In certain industries the degradation and disposal rates determine the entire organization of a product and therefore are a major part of the designs of the production plant or product. Bakeries are such an example, where bread must be eaten or destroyed within two days of manufacture, and potential sales therefore determine the output and hence the design of the production plant. It has been estimated that London hotels throw away 25 per cent of their bread purchases, endorsing the short useful life of this product. Therefore with similar products the short life cycle until disposal must be an important consideration in design and planning, and problems associated with disposal should be confronted when compiling the product design specification.

Layer 4B: Relate design disciplines to the product status

Once the product status is known, this section indicates the disciplines to be emphasized or reduced. A product which is dynamic will progress to being static and, even if dynamic, must be treated as static if only for a limited time so that a company can achieve efficient production. Similarly, a change in the environment (e.g. a technology change or government legislation) can force the status from static to dynamic again. (ST L3.2: check on the status every 6 months.)

If the product status is dynamic the disciplines under the 'product dynamic' heading in Figure 6.8 should be considered first before moving on to Static 1. If the product is static the dynamic diciplines may be ignored and work may begin on the disciplines under the heading 'Static 1'. The key to moving on to Static 2 is production volume rather than time in production (ST L4B.1), and therefore an accurate assessment of anticipated production volume is needed here (as well as in the product design specification). Note that some of the factors that make a product static or dynamic are advantages that can be emphasized (ST L4A.3).

Corfield (1979) says 'Peter Drucker saw a lot of people trying to do better that which should not be done at all'. This section should prevent that occurring.

Fourth design review (ST I.2)

A dynamic product

A product which is dynamic is being produced in an uncertain and unpredictable environment. There are likely to be many innovations and this (with few products) can justify larger research effort and costs. Applied research is the norm: non-product-related research is very unusual and was not found in our study. Dynamic products are associated with a high risk against market success, but when success is achieved a high price can be charged as it is a seller's market and a high profit will result. This is necessary to recoup the cost of design, which must continue as the product life cycle will be short.

Production is likely to be labour intensive using relatively little sophisticated production technology for short production runs. The labour used is more adaptable and has a greater general level of skill or qualifications than that involved in producing static products. This must be remembered during recruitment or retraining of personnel.

There are likely to be many small competing companies operating in a changing market. Thus marketing will be more difficult to plan and will need to be reiterative and creative (Table 6.5).

The need for sufficient attention to be given to static design

Dynamic design that ends a static plateau often results in 'bad' design. If a concept is superior to its predecessor the innovation will take the market through lower price or better performance. Within this dynamic design there may be many improvements that usually occur in the static phase concerning performance, price, quality, appearance, ergonomics, reliability, etc. The innovating company, in its

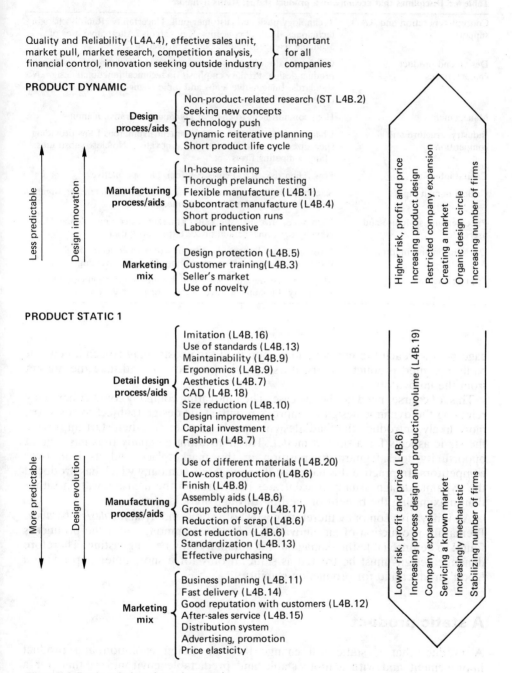

Quality and Reliability (L4A.4), effective sales unit, market pull, market research, competition analysis, financial control, innovation seeking outside industry } Important for all companies

PRODUCT DYNAMIC

Less predictable ↑

Design innovation ↑

Design process/aids {
Non-product-related research (ST L4B.2)
Seeking new concepts
Technology push
Dynamic reiterative planning
Short product life cycle

Manufacturing process/aids {
In-house training
Thorough prelaunch testing
Flexible manufacture (L4B.1)
Subcontract manufacture (L4B.4)
Short production runs
Labour intensive

Marketing mix {
Design protection (L4B.5)
Customer training(L4B.3)
Seller's market
Use of novelty

Higher risk, profit and price
Increasing product design
Restricted company expansion
Creating a market
Organic design circle
Increasing number of firms

PRODUCT STATIC 1

More predictable ↓

Design evolution ↓

Detail design process/aids {
Imitation (L4B.16)
Use of standards (L4B.13)
Maintainability (L4B.9)
Ergonomics (L4B.9)
Aesthetics (L4B.7)
CAD (L4B.18)
Size reduction (L4B.10)
Design improvement
Capital investment
Fashion (L4B.7)

Manufacturing process/aids {
Use of different materials (L4B.20)
Low-cost production (L4B.6)
Finish (L4B.8)
Assembly aids (L4B.6)
Group technology (L4B.17)
Reduction of scrap (L4B.6)
Cost reduction (L4B.6)
Standardization (L4B.13)
Effective purchasing

Marketing mix {
Business planning (L4B.11)
Fast delivery (L4B.14)
Good reputation with customers (L4B.12)
After-sales service (L4B.15)
Distribution system
Advertising, promotion
Price elasticity

Lower risk, profit and price (L4B.6)
Increasing process design and production volume (L4B.19)
Company expansion
Servicing a known market
Increasingly mechanistic
Stabilizing number of firms

Figure 6.8 Product design: dynamic to static

Table 6.5 Disciplines that accompany a product status: status dynamic

Concept generation and R&D support	Technology push and customer pull. Uncertainty. Rapidly changing techniques. Radical concepts. Key patents. Alternative uses of available science. Product design protection
Design and product characteristics	Competing design philosophies and strategies. Innovation. Major product design. Primary emphasis on technical/functional design. No standards. Imaginative leaps and rapid change. Short product life cycle
Management	High committment to change. Dynamic reiterative planning
Industry structure and competition	Changing (unpredictable) environment. Numerous firms providing specialized services. Competition innovative. No close substitutes. Many competing firms
Capital intensity	Low. High risk. R&D costs considerable, speculative
Critical human inputs	Scientific, engineering and technological. Labour-intensive, organic structure. Lateral flexible communication
Price/demand structure and user	High price, price inelastic, seller's market. Uncertainty demand high. Novelty performance and price. Exploratory user
Distribution and marketing	Close customer linkage. Uncertainty of market needs. High promotion costs. Creative marketing. Customer training
Production	Minor process design. Short runs. Limited production equipment. Flexibility. Labour intensive. Subcontract manufacture

eagerness to reach the market and recoup its design costs, may launch a new but badly designed product. Competitors may then improve it and take the market from the innovators.

This, of course, need not be the case. The innovating company could either delay releasing the dynamic design to improve it with static design (subject to costs) or, more likely, introduce the 'bad' design onto the market and then start improving the static aspects for a second model. The innovating company thus has a great opportunity to safeguard its position in the marketplace and its lead over competitors. In practice this happens: the innovative company which has produced the dynamic design usually concentrates its efforts on the next innovation rather than maximizing the benefit of the first through static design.

An innovative company therefore needs both static and dynamic *design balance*. Premature production of an innovation is far too common, and if the product is found to be unreliable the damage to the company may be long-lasting. Therefore dynamic designs must be treated as static, if only for a short time, to produce a 'good' product and for production stability.

A static product

A product that is static will change through design evolution and product improvement and with a more stable and predictable environment than for a dynamic product most forms of planning will be easier. Competition will increase but from fewer companies as mergers take place between them. These may be by horizontal integration as the more effective competition takes over the less successful, as well as by vertical integration, where companies take over some of

Table 6.6 Disciplines that accompany a product status: status Static 1

Concept generation and R&D support	Uncertainty of technology largely dispelled. Technology stabilized. Search for new product uses. Applied research for design and production back-up. Imitation of the competition
Design and product characteristics	Product improvements and new developments. Designed additions and subtractions for market segments. Pressure for standardization but with flexibility. Use of different materials. Emphasis on aesthetics and ergonomics. Design evolution. More process design than product design
Management	Business planning and control systems
Industry structure and competition	Growing competition. Pressure on prices and costs. Competition based on minor improvements in product. Casualties and mergers. Growing vertical integration
Capital intensity	Great demand for new investment. Effective purchasing
Critical human inputs	Management
Price/demand structure and user	Higher demand. Price elasticity. Price declines. Knowledge and use of the product becomes more widespread. Customers purchase more on price considerations
Distribution and marketing	Widening market. Promotion costs spread over a larger volume. Uncertainty of market largely dispelled. Increased availability. market segmentation. After-sales service network. Rapid reliable improved distribution. Emphasis on company reputation
Production	Larger volume production. Cost reduction. Capital investment. Longer runs. Product standardization. Larger batches and flow processes if applicable. Standard production techniques. Emphasis on product: finish, maintainability, size reduction, assembly aids, use of conformance standards. Reduction of scrap. CAD. Group technology

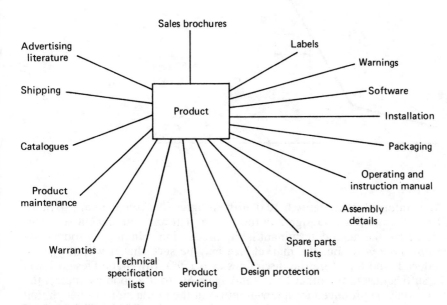

Figure 6.9 Selling checklist

their suppliers or sales outlets to secure control of their market position. There will be greater price elasticity and prices may fall. Companies can balance this fall in price by increasing demand, which will allow capital investment on improved production. This will lead to a greater standardization of the product (Table 6.6). See also Figure 6.9.

Layer 4B support text

L4B.1 The importance of production volume as opposed to time in production and the design plan

When a product is dynamic it must be treated as static for brief periods, so that production stability can be obtained. This is shown as t in Figure 6.10. The time periods t can be defined (with Sharp calculators $t = 6$ months) and production planned for maximum efficiency within this time envelope, which calls for a fast write-off of machinery and perhaps processes or, alternatively, subcontract manufacture.

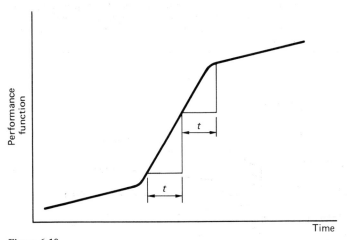

Figure 6.10

It could be inferred from Figure 6.10 that the progression from dynamic to Static Design 1 and then to Static Design 2 in the design plan was time dependent. This is partly true, but the main determinant is the production volume. A product can be static for many years but the market size may be such that it will always be batch-produced, and therefore the disciplines associated with Static Design 1 will always be sufficient. On the other hand (and again Sharp is a good example), the product may only be produced for a few months but the production volume in that time is so great that disciplines from Static 2 can be utilized. Having recognized

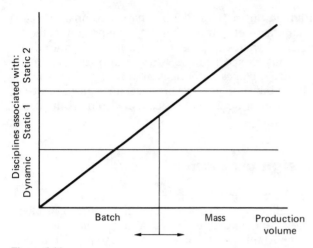

Figure 6.11

that much of the production process equipment and machinery may be written off quickly it is still viable to use these processes for this brief period (Figure 6.11).

L4B.2 Non-product-related research

This is a discipline that is associated at the earliest part of a dynamic design and may be undertaken in a university or industrial research establishment. As design is concerned with product design, non-product-related research is not strictly a design discipline but an indication of what will ultimately contribute to a dynamic design.

L4B.3 Customer training

Users are generally familiar with a well-known static product but with a dynamic product customer training may be necessary. Provision for customer training is therefore a dynamic product discipline which may enable a product to become more widely accepted and successful. Such training includes the provision of design manuals, courses of instruction and even instruction leaflets. Although these are important with static products (e.g. driving lessons) they are essential with a dynamic product where familiarity and expertise with it is unlikely to be available.

L4B.4 Subcontract manufacture

A dynamic product is subject to short production runs, in an unpredictable, changing design environment. This requires flexibility in production so that changes can be implemented quickly but without financial loss due to the obsolescence of capital equipment. One method of achieving this is through subcontract manufacture. Although this requires the purchasing company to carry the profit of the subcontract manufacturer before adding its own profit it can often be more efficient in the long run, when the product is no longer required: the supply can be discontinued, usually at short notice, with little or no cost to the purchasing company. Casio, which changes its designs annually, operates in this way. It has no manufacturing plant but sources all its products through subcontract. Subcontract manufacture is therefore a discipline associated with dynamic design and one that encourages it.

L4B.5 Patents and design protection

Although the majority of patents are taken out by large companies and are mainly concerned with small improvements to familiar products, the nature of a patent demands an invention or innovation, and it is therefore a dynamic discipline. Patents are significantly more important with a dynamic product to prevent it being imitated, thereby protecting a small company from being overtaken in the market by a non-innovative larger one with lower production costs. The more dynamic the design, the more important becomes *effective* patent protection. With a static product a company may still be successful even if it disregards small patented technological improvements which do not radically affect the basic concept and may not be clearly apparent to the customer (e.g. the recent patents on automobile piston crowns to improve air–fuel mixing). However, with a static product, as process design becomes increasingly important there is often an opportunity for patents to protect these processes.

L4B.6 Low-cost production

The selling price becomes a more important factor with a static product as it is one of the main considerations made in purchase decisions. The product, being static, is likely to be under competitive pressure and, therefore, a lower selling price can improve a company's chances of success. Although selling price should not be based on a 'cost plus' basis but should be set at a level to achieve the required market share, the minimum selling price is invariably linked to production cost. Sometimes and, in some very competitive markets, always, the selling price must be kept at the lowest possible level to win sales, which means that the production costs must be minimized. The importance of low-cost production increases in larger markets and the longer a product is static.

Low-cost production incorporates a range of disciplines that need to be emphasized with a static product (e.g. *group technology, assembly aids, cost-reduction techniques* and *reduction of scrap*). *Effective purchasing* can also reduce the overall cost of production.

With increasing volume, Static 2 disciplines become viable and these are generally aimed at lowering production costs through the introduction of *long production runs, economies of scale, automation, dedicated machinery* and *rationalization of the production range* to reduce the number of variables (preferably without reducing the customers' choice between models). Conversely, with a dynamic design it is an advantage to keep *production flexibility* to cope with likely radical changes in product design.

L4B.7 Aesthetics and fashion in design

Aesthetics is a discipline that is always dynamic or potentially so. When a product design is static the relative importance of aesthetics increases the longer it is static. For example, a new dynamic product will have little or no competition and will be purchased for its novelty, improved performance or technical advances. As time passes, and the product becomes static, competition increases as more companies manufacture a similar product using the same level of technology. To gain a competitive edge one of the opportunities open to a company is better aesthetics through appearance, style and/or the esteem perceived in ownership (status). Of course, aesthetics is more important in a 'highly visible' product (e.g. a car body) rather than an 'invisible' one (e.g. a shock absorber). However, even though appearance is less important in some products than in others, its relative importance continues to increase over time. This means that aesthetics becomes increasingly more decisive as a static discipline. It also explains why some products 'appear' to change considerably when in fact they are static (cars being a good example).

Fashion is closely linked to aesthetics in that it is always dynamic or potentially dynamic, and often is more important with a static product (e.g. clothes). For example, Ernst Thomke realized that the wristwatch was potentially a fashion item and developed the 'Swatch', a cheap, plastic but fashionable watch for SMH, the Swiss watch company.

Fashion and aesthetics should not be overlooked as a means of gaining a competitive edge with, and extending the life of, a basically static product.

L4B.8 Finish

Finish again becomes increasingly important the longer that a product is static, as it gives a visual indication of one product being better than another, which may otherwise be very similar. It is more important when the product is visual, but we have found it also to be an advantage on less visual items.

L4B.9 Ergonomics and maintainability

The term 'ergonomics' is derived from two Greek words, *ergo* (work) and *nomos* (natural law), and has been defined by Murrell (1969) as the 'scientific study of the relationship between man and his working environment'. This covers the ambient environment, tools, equipment, methods and organization of work, and in design generally it concerns ease of use with products or an environment for maximum comfort. Ergonomics is also called 'human factors' in the United States and is represented by, for example, 'User-friendly' computers.

An indication of a good ergonomic design is often a product whose use is obvious to the consumer, who will know 'instinctively' how to operate it. This may be due to compatability with existing standards or just custom and practice. An example could be an increase shown on a dial or indicator being from left to right or rotating clockwise. Another may be the position of switches to mimic equipment that users are to operate.

If designing for an international market, cultural stereotypes must be known and incorporated. For example, for electric light switches in Britain the switch is down for the 'on' position. The reverse is true in the United States and several European countries. These cultural stereotypes could become important in an emergency, when operators may revert to the expected normal operation of a mechanism. An old book, but still the bible of ergonomics, is Murrell (1969), which considers all aspects of this important area of design.

As ergonomics relies a great deal on user familiarity it is often more important with static products. However, even with dynamic designs the man/machine interface should be included in the design process. An innovative design that is unfamiliar to users will be more readily accepted if it is obvious how it should be operated (i.e. good ergonomic design).

Ergonomics and maintainability have been linked, since products that need maintenance should be designed so that this is as easy as possible. For example, parts that may require replacement during the lifetime of a product should be positioned near the surface of the product and designed for quick and easy access and installation (e.g. a pull-out/push-in circuit board or a battery replacement).

The design team should consider not only the product but also the user, who needs to perform efficiently and safely at all times. Ergonomics and maintainability can help to provide a competitive edge over companies producing similar products and, therefore, these two disciplines should be considered early in the design of a static product. As such they are disciplines mainly associated with Static 1.

L4B.10 Size reduction

When products become static there is a tendency for them to become smaller and also for their design to become more 'risky'. This is probably due to increased knowledge and experience gained with a relatively unchanging product, since the designer understands better where size and weight reduction and material savings can be introduced without jeopardizing the reliability or effectiveness of the design. Size reduction is therefore a worthwhile consideration for the design of static products.

L4B.11 Business planning

Business planning is important for both static and dynamic products but is relatively more so with static ones. Such planning is not only easier, it is likely to be more accurate when the future is much more predictable.

L4B.12 Use of reputation

Companies gain a reputation for products that have been available for a period of time and that are on a static plateau, a reputation that may be good or bad, false or true. For example, in the car market one associates Rolls-Royce with quality, Volvo with ruggedness, Porsche with fast sports cars. On the other hand, Vauxhall once had a reputation for producing 'rust boxes', and it took a long period of producing cars with better than average corrosion resistance before this reputation was laid to rest.

As a nation West Germany has provided the 'German myth' of product reliability. Having built this reputation on a few products, almost anything produced in that country is assumed to be reliable. Similarly, products from Italy are thought to have good aesthetics or to be fashionable. Companies can do the same through advertising, i.e. they can create and endorse their reputation which, of course, should be reflected in the product design. A company with a static product can promote or even create its reputation. This is therefore a static discipline.

L4B13 Use of standards in designs

This is a Static 1 discipline, and it takes two forms. Conformance standards, such as those described by the BSI, DIN, Underwriters Laboratory etc. may have to be complied with in the design of a product so that it is acceptable to a market, especially abroad, where tendering requirements require such standards to be met. Standards invariably take some time to be compiled, mainly for mass-produced items that have been available for some years. Conformance standards are therefore an indication of a static design as well as being a design discipline that is of greater importance when the product is static.

Customer 'standards' are centred on customers' familiarity with products that fit into their lifestyle and also with the need for certain products to interface with others (e.g. batteries to fit an existing radio). The need to satisfy a customer's expectations and to interface with existing products is therefore a Static 1 discipline.

L4B.14 Fast delivery, effective distribution

When a company is producing a static product using the same level of technology as the competition in order to gain an advantage it can incorporate certain static disciplines. Fast delivery, getting products to customers more quickly than the competition and quoting and fulfilling short lead times involves a large area of physical distribution management, sales organization, production scheduling and management. More recently, automation and computerized inventory control have led to improvements in this area which are both easier to achieve and are likely to be more effective with a static product serving a known market.

L4B.15 After-sales service

With a static product an effective after-sales service network (where necessary) can result in a greater likelihood of repurchase by users. To be effective, there needs to be good service training and the provision of tools, equipment and knowledge. Such an infrastructure takes time and expense to set up, and therefore to justify set-up costs it will be necessary to have a static design. A dynamic design is unlikely to have the performance consistency to justify such a network. An after-sales service network is therefore a static discipline that can be used to improve a company's competitive edge.

L4B.16 Imitation and imitators

The period during which many products are dynamic is often brief, and this is then followed by a static phase. Innovating companies not only cause the product to become dynamic, they must often try to keep it so in order to survive and not be overtaken by other companies with low-cost production and static design. In traditional markets the static phase has often been sufficiently long to make most of the companies in these markets (and often those that dominate) unable to change effectively, either through their reliance on dedicated machinery and low-cost production or lack of suitable personnel. These companies rely on a stable environment.

Between these two extremes are companies that are prepared to adopt a dynamic design that has recently become static. They operate at a static level, but in the realization that it is often an artificial constraint, in order to maximize production efficiency. These companies are imitators. They have the ability to recognize and benefit from innovation without themselves being the innovators. They appreciate the potential of an innovation which may be too expensive for the main market but which can be improved through static design. Such companies can lower the price, thus creating or expanding the market and often taking it over from the originators.

The imitators therefore require extensive market research and an organic organizational structure that can cope with change. The apparent dichotomy is that manufacture must be low cost but also flexible to maximize static design and to adapt to a changing environment. This suggests a practice of subcontract manufacture or a flexible manufacturing system that can be programmed to allow for changes in production.

Design protection is not so important but avoidance of the innovators' design protection ('beating patents') can be crucial to the imitator's success. The main threat to imitators is competition from other imitators.

L4B.17 Group technology

The term 'group technology' has been used in two contexts when referring to the organization of a factory. In the late 1960s and early 1970s it was used to describe the work system initiated at the Volvo car plant in Sweden, where assembly workers were organized into groups or cells to assemble the entire vehicle. This was believed to overcome the 'anomie' or 'loss of meaning' that was present in the more common car product assembly line, where workers more usually assembled a few components in a highly repetitive cycle, often beside a conveyor system. Measurable improvements were claimed in product quality through group technology. This technique was overtaken by a technology where many of the repetitive tasks previously undertaken by manual labour are now done by machines, and even at Volvo this system has been abandoned at their newer plant (Kalmar). This form of group technology may still be applicable to dynamic products which have not stabilized in their design sufficiently to justify investment in the production technology.

The second context in which group technology operates has its roots in the 1950s, where, initially, machines were positioned to improve production flow through the plant but then developed so that components, or assemblies, could be grouped together or rationalized across several products. This practice is still widely applicable today, but it can only operate satisfactorily with static products. Group technology in this form is therefore a static discipline.

L4B.18 CAD and CAM

Pugh and Smith (1976) have reported how CAD will 'have the highest utilization' when used for products at the conventional boundary where there is 'a minimum of synthesis in broad terms' and designs are 'centred around developments based on well proven concepts'. This theory has been further expanded in Pugh (1983, 1984), showing conclusively that CAD is likely to be more useful in the design of static products. Therefore CAD is a static discipline.

Pugh (1984) has described how CAD/CAM systems originated from manufacturing considerations rather than from product design, and that these have been most successfully used where the concept is fixed (Pugh, 1985). Therefore CAM is also a static discipline.

Several interviewees argued that CAD was being used for dynamic design, but, when questioned further, they agreed that this was only for special tasks in certain narrow areas of dynamic design. Pugh (1985) has stated that CAD systems 'are extremely cumbersome to use even in staccato mode – both from the hardware and software viewpoints'. CAD and CAM, as currently configured, are therefore static disciplines in design.

L4B.19 The change of emphasis from product design to process design

Allied to the design of products is that of their method of manufacture. In the following we will discuss this process design and point out where it becomes dominant over product design.

Process design is the design of the method of manufacture rather than of the actual product. Possibly the earliest form of process design was prescribed by Taylor (1911), who described the optimization of tools (and operators) in the production process: 'Get an ox to do an ox's work.'

Throughout the twentieth century various practitioners have continued to ascribe methods for increasing production from employees (e.g. Gilbreth and Gilbreth, 1916; Fayol, 1949; Mayo, 1933; Herzberg et al, 1959). More recently, with increases in automation, research has been directed away from maximizing the individual operator's output to maximizing output from the manufacturing process, resulting in considerable process design. It has been estimated that in certain industries, such as tinned foods, more is spent on process design than product design. There are various aspects of process design and these are discussed and proposed where and when they become useful in the design process (Layers 4B and 5).

As the design of a product becomes static, process design often becomes more important than product design, as stability in product design makes investment in the manufacturing process more viable. The relative change from product to process design has been known for some years, as Usher (1929) noted when considering the design of lathes in the nineteenth century: 'At a late stage in the total process of achievement, the conceptual or saltatory elements had become subordinate in importance to critical revision in execution and construction' (p.330).

This increasing relative importance of process design has been observed by Abernathy and Utterback (1978) and described by Foxall (1984):

> The transition from the small, highly technological, entrepreneurial unit to the established, high volume productive unit represents a key pivoted point in the innovative process and occurs when a dominant product design becomes available. As each project won acceptance, its productive unit increased in size and concentrated its innovation on improving production (p.28).

Only recently has significant research been put into this direction with the work of such people as Taguchi (1985), now being followed in the West.

Johne (1985) includes Figure 6.12, which demonstrates that process innovation

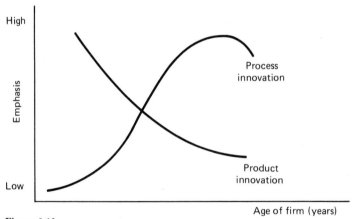

Figure 6.12

increases as product innovation decreases, although he shows the base of the graph to be the age of the firm rather than that of the product, perhaps overlooking the fact that a firm may have several products, some of which may be quite new. He appears to be describing a single-product company. Even so, the trend is clear that, over time, process innovation is more emphasized than product innovation. Once process design dominates, it is often quite difficult to reverse the sequence, as the process that makes a firm more productive tends to make it less flexible and less inventive.

However, product design must not cease completely during this period, although its emphasis will probably be on incremental improvements, as shown by Deasley (1986):

To maintain good economic performance, industry must employ two innovative routes in its manufacturing business:

Product Management, i.e. continued and critical up-dating during all stages of product life.

Competitive Manufacture, i.e. continual seeking of best practice in terms of quality and cost.

That is, in the terms of this book, continued static product design and increasing process design. The key to the increase in process design is production volume, which is discussed in more detail in ST L4B.1.

L4B.20 The use of different materials in design

This is similar to aethetics in that it is always dynamic but becomes more important the longer a product is static. Therefore it is mainly a static discipline. New materials may, of course, be important in or be the very nature of a dynamic design such as those used as the basis of microprocessors or superconductors. More commonly, new materials can be constantly investigated in a static design to improve performance of various parameters such as reducing cost, lowering weight, improving the temperature range, improving strength, reducing corrosion and improving the production or appearance of the product. Investigating and using new materials can therefore enhance and improve the marketability of a product without altering its existing concept.

Layer 5: Static 2 disciplines

When the production rate reaches a certain volume a new set of disciplines comes into play, and these are shown in Figure 6.13. This production volume varies depending on the product, and is that which is sufficient to recoup the investment made on these new disciplines, with profit, over the product's lifetime. This lifetime may be the point at which an incremental change is made (e.g. new press tools, a change of car model) or, in some cases, at the end of a static plateau.

Although disciplines from Static 2 can be used on a dynamic product (ST L4B.1) they will generally only be suitable with a static one (Figure 6.14). Whatever improvement in performance function (X) is made for a static or dynamic product it can be seen that the time available to recoup the investment with a static product (t_s) is much greater than with a dynamic one (t_o) and therefore, except for a few multinational companies, the disciplines associated with Static 2 are viable only with static products.

Static 2 products

A product which is a static design is being produced in a stable and predictable environment. There are few innovations associated with this product as technology will have stabilized and less risk is attached to its marketing, which is far better understood than with dynamic or newly static products. Furthermore, the producers understand their position in this market, whether they are market leader, imitator or seeking a safe market niche away from the major competitors. Conversely, there is a small profit margin and high profits must be generated by a large volume of sales. Profit, though, can be improved by the economies of scale which can be increasingly introduced with a product that has a long product life cycle.

Operating at this level generally means that the production methods are capital intensive where it becomes viable to invest large sums in production technology to reduce the unit cost of the product often by only a very small amount. Similarly, a small saving in the manufactured cost of the product through a static design change can often result in a large capital return. Swan Vesta are reported to have saved millions by the simple expediency of putting the match-striking face on only one side of the box, where previously it was on both.

For Static 2 products competition is usually fierce from the few competitors and it is often a buyer's market especially if the product is reaching market saturation as it has in Europe with cars, washing machines, televisions and other consumer durables. Products that have reached this stage of their life are often having an impact on society, and may become subject to the attention of governments as a source of revenue through taxation or curbs if considered unhealthy (e.g. alcohol and cigarettes). With certain very large industries the products can be used to help stimulate or depress the entire economy (e.g. the 'stop – go' British industry of the 1960s). Companies must become aware of these political considerations if they are operating at this level.

Although there will be a long product life cycle with such products there is often a planned short model life cycle. Every two or three years small static changes are made to the design, often a change in the aesthetics, improved ergonomics or 'add-on' features (e.g. a new colour range for saucepans, a sunshine roof in a car, or a

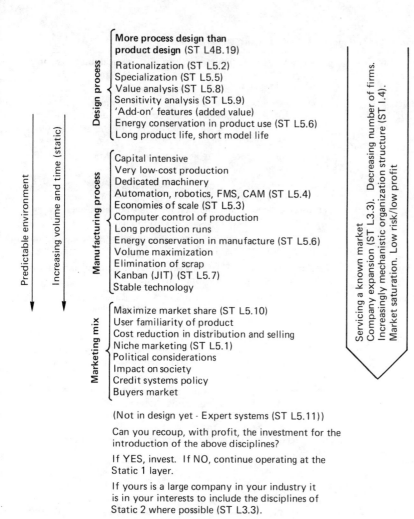

Design process {
More process design than
product design (ST L4B.19)
Rationalization (ST L5.2)
Specialization (ST L5.5)
Value analysis (ST L5.8)
Sensitivity analysis (ST L5.9)
'Add-on' features (added value)
Energy conservation in product use (ST L5.6)
Long product life, short model life
}

Manufacturing process {
Capital intensive
Very low-cost production
Dedicated machinery
Automation, robotics, FMS, CAM (ST L5.4)
Economies of scale (ST L5.3)
Computer control of production
Long production runs
Energy conservation in manufacture (ST L5.6)
Volume maximization
Elimination of scrap
Kanban (JIT) (ST L5.7)
Stable technology
}

Marketing mix {
Maximize market share (ST L5.10)
User familiarity of product
Cost reduction in distribution and selling
Niche marketing (ST L5.1)
Political considerations
Impact on society
Credit systems policy
Buyers market
}

Predictable environment

Increasing volume and time (static)

Servicing a known market
Company expansion (ST L3.3). Decreasing number of firms.
Increasingly mechanistic organization structure (ST I.4).
Market saturation. Low risk/low profit.

(Not in design yet - Expert systems (ST L5.11))

Can you recoup, with profit, the investment for the introduction of the above disciplines?

If YES, invest. If NO, continue operating at the Static 1 layer.

If yours is a large company in your industry it is in your interests to include the disciplines of Static 2 where possible (ST L3.3).

Figure 6.13 Product design: Static 2 disciplines

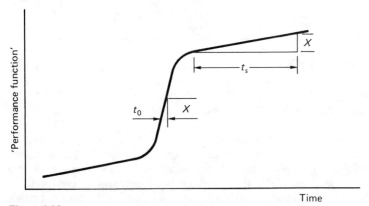

Figure 6.14

Table 6.7 Disciplines that accompany a product status: status Static 2

Concept generation and R&D support	Few innovations. Technology stabilized. Technical solutions known. Continuing emphasis on cost saving. Increased concern with behavioural aspects
Design and product characteristics	Product attributes known. Design for minimum user cost. Minor product design. Stress on cost of design and its effectiveness. Use of standards. 'Model' changes. Value analyses. Energy conservation in product use. Process design patents
Management	Political considerations may become important. Management and financial systems. Attention to group size
Industry structure and competition	Market saturation. Specialization. Substitutes prevalent. Number of firms declining. Fierce competition. Large companies may yield sufficient economies of scale to drive rivals out of business. market segmentation. Stable (predictable) environment
Capital intensity	High due to large quantity of specialized equipment. Major inward cash flow. Low risk/low profit
Critical human inputs	Engineering personnel. Unskilled, semi-skilled labour. mechanistic structure most appropriate. Specialization
Price/demand structure and user	Inelastic demand. Customer sophistication. Buyer's market. Information easily available. Impact on society. Sales growth slows. Financial credit systems policy
Distribution and marketing	Stability of market needs. Market attributes known. Niche marketing. market saturation. Product 'images' for designed features of quality, etc. Seeking large market share. Emphasis on purchasers' lifestyle and user appeal
Production	Application of computers. Long runs and stable technology. Capital intensive. Very low cost production. Mass production. Synergy. Economies of scale. Emphasis on: automation, robotics/FMS/CAM, energy conservation in production. Dedicated machinery. 'Just in time'. Rationalization of the product range. Specialization by workforce.

new styled cabinet for a television set). Static design in these areas can be planned with marketing and can continue to give a new appeal to customers without basically altering the design of a product being produced at Static 2 (Table 6.7).

Layer 5 support text

L5.1 Niche marketing

When a dynamic product is introduced onto the market it is generally priced highly as users are prepared to pay for the product's improvement in performance and/ or novelty. The pressure from competition is likely to be low, as are available production quantities. However, as the product becomes static, competition increases, production volume grows and the relative price falls as the product gains wider acceptance. When products are on the static plateau most manufacturers will aim them at the largest section of the mass market. However, companies, and especially the smaller, less successful ones that cannot command sufficient economies of scale, will increasingly seek out market niches. By studying parametric analysis (ST L4A.4) clustering occurs of products aimed at the area perceived as the main market. As this area becomes saturated with producers, more companies seek market niches on the fringes of the production parameters, where competition will be less and relatively higher prices may be charged. Niche marketing, and therefore designing to meet these market niches, is a Static 2 discipline.

L5.2 Rationalization

This takes two forms, both of which are applicable only in the manufacture of a static product design. From a marketing aspect, companies endeavour to match their products to certain segments of the market and eliminate, or reduce, those products which appear to be serving the same market and are competing for the same customers. This often occurs after a merger (a sign of a static product in itself) between companies, where follows a pruning of two competing product ranges into what is believed to be one superior range.

Where possible, within a company few variations in components are used right across the product range. If this can be achieved there is a significant saving through economies of scale, bulk purchasing, reduction of stock and ancilliary paperwork such as drawings. In our research one company had managed to rationalize on door handles so that one handle design was used throughout the product range. Rationalization in this context can only be achieved if the product is static and, furthermore, can actually prevent a product becoming dynamic if this rationalization is strictly adhered to. Rationalization is therefore a static discipline.

L5.3 Economies of scale

As the term suggests, economies of scale are savings in cost that can be achieved solely through mass producing a large number of similar items. Machine usage is greatly increased and therefore, with less idle time, machines become more viable. Automation can be introduced which can reduce labour costs, and the unit cost of tooling is greatly reduced by having its cost spread over a very large number of components. The purchasing department is able to command much better prices through bulk purchases, and the cost of drawings, purchase orders, designs, research and development and other fixed costs can be spread over a larger number of items.

As production increases more effective technology can be introduced, for example from centre lathe turning, to capstan lathe, from chucking auto to multi-spindle auto, and, provided the market can absorb the higher volumes of output, the unit cost will decline. However, this is a step function and not a linear decline in costs. There are also savings to be made to the unit cost of the product in distribution, selling outlets, advertising and servicing.

If a product is on a static plateau and the production volume is sufficient to justify disciplines from Static 2 it is important to maximize the economies of scale in order to stay competitive in a fiercely competitive market.

L5.4 Automation

When the design process was shown to design managers, some disagreed with the statement that CAD and automation were static design discipline and, furthermore, were an indication that a product was static.

Automation, in its present form, be it robotics, flexible manufacturing system (FMS), computer-controlled machinery centres or CAM, is advertised as being easily reprogrammable to the point where it is possible to use it for 'one-offs'. In theory this may be the case, but in practice it is unlikely to occur at present. Part of the reason for this is that the purchase of automation needs to be justified, and this is based on return on investment (historical accounting). This justification is likely to be made on the saving from the manufacture of a product or perhaps a few similar products. Therefore there needs to be some confidence in the firm that these products will continue to be made for some time in the future.

We found that a commonly expressed view among design managers was that accountants must learn that automated systems were, as one person put it, 'not like buying one press tool for one job' but should be thought of 'as part of the building', because it is 'easy to change the product'. This may be the case, but at present the justification for automation seems to be made in the same way as for a press tool, and practice bears this out. Automation is currently used almost exclusively by companies mass producing similar products which they intend to continue making in a similar form over the next few years.

Another reason for automation being an indicator of a static product is that the nature of automation, as it exists at present, is not as flexible as suppliers would wish us to believe. An example given to us was that flexible systems are such that any engine size could be programmed to be assembled into a car on an automated production system – as long as the engine mounts were the same. To take this a step further, robot welding equipment, for example, may be reprogrammed to weld different products but it can only weld. Therefore this limits the designer's freedom to innovate a replacement product, which may require a different method for joining the parts and therefore a different type of robot, thus rendering the robot obsolete before it has reached the end of its (book) life.

Therefore automation is a static discipline and an indication that a product is static at this time. It is anticipated that in the future, with a more widespread acceptance of dynamic accounting, relatively lower cost automation and a greater degree of flexibility from systems, automation will no longer be a static discipline.

L5.5 Worker specialization

As a Static 2 discipline, specialization of workers making a product becomes more important. The longer a product is static, the more experience can be used in its design and production. Also the production volumes may be such that individuals can specialize in one particular facet of its manufacture. This would not be possible with a dynamic product, where the environment and the product will change too rapidly to enable employees to be skilled in just one feature of the product or its manufacture. This is also related to a mechanistic design team structure which is operable through a set of rules and may be considered as a 'subcontract' within an organization. Some employees may operate within these 'subcontracted' skills who can only work with a product whose design is static and is likely to remain so for some considerable time.

L5.6 Energy conservation

This is a Static 2 discipline associated with products that are manufactured in large quantities and over a longer period of time. It takes two forms:

1. *Energy conservation in production.* This entails seeking the most energy-efficient use of production equipment, matching a machine's performance closely to that actually required in the machining operation (e.g. using a press which has a maximum capacity just above that required to do the pressing operation), avoiding unnecessarily long transport between various stages of production, insulating the factory, etc. All this is aimed to make a plant more energy efficient.
2. *Energy conservation in the product.* This involves enabling the customers to reduce their operating costs and makes the product more attractive to them, thereby affecting their purchase decision. This is probably a Static 2 discipline as it is unlikely that, with anything other than a mass-produced product, the user will be aware of the running costs associated with a product. One example is the petrol consumption figures for cars in which great emphasis is laid in advertisements on those models that use less fuel. Another is the Roberts radio once chosen by *Which?*, the consumer magazine, as being the 'best buy', the deciding factor being its very low consumption of batteries.

L5.7 Just in time (Kanban)

Much has been written in periodicals, and stated at conferences, about the advantages to be gained from the introduction of 'just-in-time' (JIT). This has been defined as 'A philosophy directed towards the elimination of waste, where waste is anything which adds cost, but not value to a product' (*Engineering Computers*, Vol. 3, No.5, September 1986).

JIT was developed in Japan by the Toyota Car Company, who observed that in American supermarkets the shelves were restocked as they became depleted rather than being loaded with several weeks' supply of any one product. Most commonly, suppliers deliver components when they are required on the day and sometimes on the hour. The advantage of this to the manufacturer is a reduction of stockholding and therefore warehousing costs and a fast turnover of inventory. The former chairman of Ford, Sam Toy, told the authors how a new press shop at Dagenham had been sited in a building that was previously used for holding stocks from their suppliers, and that this space had been made available entirely due to the introduction of JIT.

JIT has only been possible in Britain with the stabilization of union/management-relations and the reduction of stoppages in the 1980s compared to the industrial strife of the 1970s. This has been linked with the increased study of Japanese manufacturing practices by organizations in both Europe and the USA. JIT can only work with effective quality control practices which ensure that products that leave the factory and are received by the customers (who may themselves be manufacturers) are to specification and are free from fault. Second, a prerequisite for effective JIT is 'a repetitive manufacturing environment' (Huckerby, 1988), which indicates a static product design or a dynamic product design produced in very large quantities.

JIT is essentially linked to computerized manufacturing for fast, accurate processing of management systems, including capacity planning and scheduling, inventory control and sales order processing. Although the price of such systems is falling, it is still prohibitive for most small companies. The cost can only be justified by large companies certain of production stability for some time in the future – again, those with a static product design.

JIT can work within any company in respect of reducing work in progress, elimination of production bottlenecks and reducing setting up and waiting time, but the most widely discussed saving derived from JIT, that of 'daily' component supply, is available only to large manufacturers. For example, a small manufacturer may only need small quantities of components, which it will be unable to order in quantities large enough to make daily delivery viable. Therefore the manufacturer will still need to hold stocks of components. Furthermore, it may not have the 'muscle' to demand daily component deliveries, which must be an added expense to suppliers who would prefer to make just one large delivery.

A company supplying another company operating JIT will need to hold buffer stocks to ensure continuity of delivery in the event of some unforseen circumstance (e.g. faulty material, late delivery from their suppliers or industrial action). In other words, small companies must operate as a warehouse for their larger customers and suppliers. This major part of JIT is therefore a Static 2 discipline available only to mass producers.

L5.8 Value analysis

Value analysis is defined as 'a systematic inter-disciplinary examination of factors affecting the cost of a product or service, in order to devise means of achieving the specified purpose most economically at the required standard of quality and reliability' (BSI *Design Management Systems*, Forthcoming). It should be acceptable only to Static 2 although, in practice, it is used earlier. When savings are quoted as having been made through value analysis it is worth questioning why the design was not done like that in the first place. Value analysis does not usually change the concept of a product but seeks to simplify and cost reduce the existing concept: therefore it is a static discipline. If the product has been correctly designed in the first place value analysis should yield little. However, over a period of time, and with increasing production volumes, different materials, methods and production techniques become viable and relative costs between components change, which makes value analysis of even well-designed products worthwhile. Value analysis is therefore a discipline associated with Static 2.

The evidence of our interview results showed that value analysis was often used, indicating that the original design put into production was not as effective as it should have been.

L5.9 Sensitivity analysis

The form this takes is similar to that of value analysis, but in this efforts made in the design changes are directed towards those areas where there are the greatest potential savings. For example, if, in the overall cost of a product, the screws cost 0.2 per cent and the castings 10 per cent, one must direct design changes towards the castings and not spend time on trying to save on the cost of screws. This form of analysis is common in the petrochemical industry but would be equally useful in other industries. Like value analysis, it is a discipline associated with Static 2.

L5.10 The importance of market share

We found that almost all the people that we interviewed in our study thought that market share was less important than seeking a profitable segment of that market. The one exception was in the most successful of all the companies in the study, and this may not be merely coincidence. Several writers have indicated the advantage of a large market share: 'It has been shown that companies with the highest market share tend to have the highest profit margins' (Schoeffler *et al.*, 1974). Oxenfeldt (1959) also noted its importance: 'Increases in market share are closely associated with increases in profitability, improved chances of survival, and minimizing the risk of loss.'

It has been noted that Western companies are orientated towards short-term profitability whereas Japanese marketing concentrates on market share. In a survey of British and Japanese companies by Doyle *et al.* (1985), 87 per cent of Japanese companies gave 'aggressive growth' or 'market domination' as their objective but only 20 per cent of those targets applied to British companies. 'Maintaining the status quo' and 'preventing decline' were the most typical British objective: 'The British were willing to allow their market position to be eroded in order to obtain short term profitability.' However, as Doyle *et al.* also note, 'a company can improve profitability by raising volume or by cutting costs or by improving productivity' – all three can be linked to market share.

A large market share allows a company greater freedom to obtain the benefits of economies of scale in production, with better machine utilization and rationalization and with larger purchases of materials and components. The company can also benefit from more viable selling outlets and relatively lower research and development and advertising costs. Learning curves also show that the more of any one product a plant manufactures (and the more familiar the producers become with that product), the more efficient they become, thereby reducing the unit cost of production.

Large market share, therefore, is an important aim in static product design, and achieving it is one of the disciplines for Static 2 in the design plan.

L5.11 Expert systems

The genesis of expert systems and their application lies in geology and medicine, and, in both cases, they are used in diagnostic roles. The earliest recorded application was by Shortliffe (1976), who designed a computer-based medical consultation system called MYCĪN, and it was after this that people have tried to apply such systems to design, with varying degrees of success.

Dixon and Simmons (1983) state that Brown and Chandrasekaran's (1983) paper was the first attempt to apply the existing technology of expert systems to mechanical design, and in the same year Ellas (1983) considered the possibility of using expert systems in aircraft design. However, as Dixon and Simmons state:

> Engineering design is an ill-structured problem; that is, it lacks a well defined goal ... Different designs will come up with different solutions ... all meeting the specification.

At present, expert systems are suitable only for staccato use and generally in the design of static products. However, if, as the literature states, they are really to be artificial intelligence, capable of generating new concepts, they should be associated with dynamic design.

Part of the failure of expert systems, for use in design, is due to the hitherto lack of structure and procedure in the actual design process. Designers of expert systems do not know what to design, or in fact what design entails. Although expert systems are 'inference engines', they still rely on experience when they are being programmed. The design process will give structure and procedure, but it is not developed in a form that could be used efficiently as a basis for an expert system.

How does this relate to product status? If we look again at the medical analogy the design of man has evolved over millions of years. He can be classified as a static concept. Although we did not design him, we are starting to tinker with his subsystem and component design (i.e. organ replacements, artificial knee joints, etc.). Therefore the medical and geological systems have been arrived at diagnostically and are used diagnostically, *not* generatively, and they are used to some effect because the concept is static. In medicine we do not have the three-headed, four-legged, six-armed man that we would see regularly in engineering. So what is to be done?

It is not quite so bad as Dixon and Simmons (1983) believe since, for truly static concepts (permanent), it could be quite safe and useful to devise an expert system (diagnostically) and then use it generatively for designing another version of the same device (i.e. scale up, scale down, conceptual and subsystem variations almost zero, components variable).

The differential gear is, as far as can be proven, a truly static concept in that it was first used by the Chinese on a chariot in 2600 BC and, conceptually, it is identical to that used in today's cars. Although these gears do not have wooden teeth, millions of dollars and man-hours have been invested in refining their technology. Therefore for devices of this type it may be safe to establish and use an expert system generatively. For most products, particularly those that are truly dynamic, expert systems as currently configured will never be able to handle the truly open-ended situation – but they cope with subsystems if these are static.

Edosomwan (1987) provides a good summary of the current state of the applications in his ten design rules for KBES (Knowledge Based Expert Systems). He has the user very much in mind:

1. Obtain the right knowledge base.
2. Form knowledge-base procedure.
3. Provide adequate structure for systems prompts and human socialization.
4. Provide adequate KBES response time.

5. Provide adequate explanations and documentation for all system variables.
6. Provide adequate KBES time-sharing options.
7. Provide adequate user interface on KBES.
8. Provide intersystem communication ability.
9. Provide automatic programming ability and controls on KBES.
10. Provide flexibility for ongoing maintenance and update of KBES.

Edosomwan focuses on the consistent, repetitive task as being the basis for success – thus supporting the view that truly static products are the only ones to lend themselves to expert systems.

Perhaps a final comment on the current position was made by a manufacturer of fuel injection systems to a member of the Alvey project. They stated that expert systems could not have generated any of their ten fuel injection pump concepts then under consideration (Marquis, 1986). Therefore, for such rarities as the differential gear, which may be said to be truly static, expert systems could be considered a static discipline. However, for most products they are not yet a viable discipline.

Part 3

7 A worked example of the system

We now show an example of the use of the system in a hypothetical company, who are considering a new product. The company, Omega Wire Forming plc, is the largest of its kind in the country (Figure 7.1). It uses much specialized production equipment and its main products are springs and wire clips that are supplied to the automotive industry. However, its output is falling as a result of the decline in the UK automotive industry.

3 January 1989: Memo to Market Research, Production, Sales Managers and Design Manager, from Board of Directors
This company has a commitment to constantly updating its product range and we are now seeking a new product to enter production twelve months from this date. This new product must realize an annual turnover of over £100 000 and repay the cost of design and development (including tooling), in no longer than three years. With our current minimum gross margin requirements of 20 per cent, the total cost to be in production must not exceed, for example, £60 000 for a product with a £100 000 annual turnover.

Although it should be borne in mind that, being the largest wire forming company in the UK, we have experience with wire drawn products and excess capacity of wire forming machinery, there is no restriction on the type of new product provided that it fulfils the above requirements.

Design Manager, please form a design circle.

The above memo covers the *Preliminary Layer* giving some management design requirements. There is management commitment to design as well as an initial financial control over it. It will be seen that design is fairly restricted by the conditions laid down.

Proceed to Layer 1: Product definition

16 January 1989: Memo to Design Manager, Sales Manager, Production Manager and Accountant, from Market Research Manager
I have discussed the Director's memo with those in my department [Organic Design] and our apprentice suggests that there may be an opportunity in the market for paper clips, or something similar, as our new product. I have prepared the Product Definition for your consideration.

PRODUCT DEFINITION – TITLE: PAPER CLIP
Product purpose
To hold up to six papers together as a temporary fastening. The papers must be easily withdrawn from the paper clip without damage to either the paper or the clip.

135

136

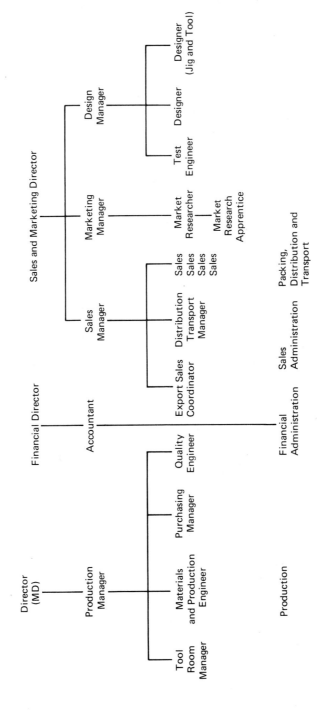

Figure 7.1 Organization chart of Omega Wire Forming plc

Market
Stationery markets (e.g. offices, schools and home use).

Why there is a need
The price of paper clips has risen, apparently unnecessarily, by 20 per cent in the past two years, which is well ahead of inflation. The cost of the wire of that gauge has risen by 7 per cent in the past two years. In spite of this and the 'paperless office', demand has risen constantly over the past five years by about 5 per cent. It is believed that the product is purchased entirely on price and the competitors are following the market leader, who has made this product apparently a very profitable item. It is felt that, with no apparent customer loyalty to any particular brand, we could achieve a satisfactory profit and market share.

Competition
Staples, and perhaps glue, may be considered competition but these are a more permanent form of fastening which can only be used once and will damage the paper. Bulldog type clips are widely used but these cost twenty times the price of a paper clip and are not directly in competition.

Competitors
Bloggs Paper Clips plc is the market leader with 40–45 per cent of the UK market. Ajax BV of Holland are the world's largest manufacturers with 10–20 per cent of the UK market and perhaps 10 per cent of world markets.

   The following companies each have around 10 per cent of the UK market: Alpha, Beta, Gamma, Delta. These all make the familiar type of paper clip except Delta, who produce a larger plastic type of clip which sometimes has a company name or logo stamped on it for promotional use.

Anticipated demand price
If these can be produced at three for a penny (at prices 1.1.89) an estimated demand of 10 per cent of the UK market, which is 500 million/year, could be achieved (50 million). One of the main costs incurred is anticipated to be the distribution.

   If the price can be reduced to four for one penny we could expect a UK demand of around 80 million and a possible export potential for a further 20 million if distribution costs are low enough.

Question: Does the design project suit your management requirements?

Option A: 50 million paper clips at 3/p = annual turnover of £165000
Option B: 100 million paper clips at 4/p = annual turnover of £250000

Total design and development costs allowed:

Option A: 20% gross margin on £165000 turnover = £33000
   Maximum design and development cost = 3 years × 33000 = £99000
Option B: 20% gross margin on £250000 turnover = £50000
   Maximum design and development cost = 3 years × 50000 = £150000

Maximum development time twelve months (not known)

   At this stage the product appears to fulfil the management requirements regarding turnover, but insufficient information is available to confirm the design and development costs or the development time.

Answer: At this stage, yes.

Question: Does the anticipated demand suit your company's production equipment?

2 February 1989: Memo to Accountant, Market Research Manager, Sales Manager and Design Manager, from Production Manager
Not wishing to pre-empt the final design I can confirm that if the familiar design is to be manufactured the project appears, at this stage, to be viable from a production point of view. The type of machinery to be used is already installed and underutilized. Tooling will be between £20000 and £30000 and should last for about 100 million paper clips.

The annual output of 50 million clips can be produced on one machine operating 16 hours a day in 209 days, which allows plenty of days for maintenance, holidays or breakdown.

The annual output of 100 million could also be produced on one machine working 20 hours a day in 334 days which is getting a bit tight, but as this production output will build up gradually I believe we will be able to accommodate it.

A rough cost breakdown is shown below:

50 million: anticipated selling price = 0.3p (allowing 0.033p for distribution)
           0.3p less 20% gross margin = 0.24p (A)

(1) Unit material cost   = 0.100p
(2) Unit machining cost   = 0.067p
(3) Unit tooling cost   = 0.025p
                            _____
   Total manufacturing cost = 0.192p   (A) 0.24p

(This is a simplified sum to demonstrate the principle.)

100 million: anticipated selling price = 0.22p (allowing 0.03 for distribution)
            0.22p less 20% gross margin = 0.176p (B)

(4) Unit material cost   = 0.080p
    Unit machining cost   = 0.067p
    Unit tooling cost   = 0.025p
                            _____
   Total manufacturing cost = 0.172p   (B) 0.176p

(The 100 million option looks doubtful. Export is therefore unlikely with the higher distribution costs.)

1. A standard paper clip uses 10cm of finished wire which costs, on a purchase of 5 million metres annually, a unit price of 0.1p.
2. The machine to be used can produce 15000 paper clips an hour and has a running cost of £10/hour. Unit cost per paper clip = 0.67p.
3. 100 million clips on a tooling cost of £25000 unit cost per paper clip = 0.025p.
4. With 10 million metres the unit price falls to 0.08p.

We have produced tooling similar to this previously and the time for its design and manufacture in the tool room takes about three months with another two months testing to iron out snags. The Design Manager agrees with this estimate.

Answer: Yes.

Question: Does the product suit your company's sales and distribution?

2 February 1989: Memo to Accountant, Market Research Manager, Design Manager and Production Manager, from Sales Manager
We currently do not have the necessary system for sales and distribution, but at this stage I do not foresee any significant problem. The fall in demand for our other products has left some surplus capacity in our transport department which can be diverted for the distribution of paper clips.

A preliminary investigation has shown that the most likely method of distribution will be central warehouses, such as Brown's plc, who accept the consignment then package and deliver them to stationers under their own label.

My initial estimate is that we will have to deliver weekly which will cost, at the very outside, £330 for a delivery of one million or £600 for a delivery of two million. I have supplied these figures to the Production Manager to aid his estimate. Distribution to a European warehouse will be over £2000 for a delivery of two million paper clips.

Answer: No, but it is worth adapting the firm.

Question: Do you have the experience, expertise and technology needed for this market?

Answer: On the familiar design, yes for product design and production. On the sales side, it can be obtained as far as can be judged at this stage.

Memo from Board of Directors to Design Manager
This project takes priority over all other design projects currently in progress.

First design review

Proceed to layer 2: Status specification

2 April 1989: Memo to Sales Manager, Production Manager and Design Manager, from Marketing Manager
Competition analysis
The pricing and demand identified in the product definition has been further investigated and found to be current. A more accurate breakdown of current market shares is given below:

	Market share in year (%)		
	1986	1987	1988
Bloggs plc	50	48	48
Ajax BV	10	14	20
Alpha plc	15	18	15
Beta Ltd	10	7	6
Gamma Ltd	5	6	6
Delta plc	5	5	5
Naff plc	5	2	0
	100	100	100

Naff plc has ceased trading.

Nearly all the paper clips appear to be the same with the exception of Delta, who produce a large flat plastic clip and these cost twice as much as the other competitors' products. It is confirmed that there is no customer loyalty to any particular make.

Bloggs, Ajax and Alpha produce epoxy-painted coloured clips which sell for 50 per cent more than their standard finish. The 'standard' sized clip accounts for in excess of 90 per cent of demand.

Customers appear to be happy with the existing design except that there are some complaints that clips have sharp ends that can scratch the paper when the clip is removed. Some are difficult to apply to the paper and clips can be a problem if they fall into photocopiers or other office machines.

Market research
There are no relevant conformance standards concerning the paper clip design. There is legislation as to the cadmium finish used on some clips which prevent their use in

Scandinavia and similar legislation has been proposed for the EEC. Most companies use a nickel-plate finish and a few brass, which is acceptable in all countries. The plastic clips are polypropylene on which there is no restriction as to their use.

The wire used is readily available at a viable price.

The increase in the service industry is the reason for the (confirmed) 5 per cent annual increase in demand and this trend (in spite of the 'paperless office') is expected to continue.

The distribution system is well established from central warehouses, as is the method of packaging being carried out at these warehouses. It is not anticipated that any new design would need to affect this infrastructure. There is no servicing or after-sales service needed for paper clips.

There is no safety legislation concerning paper clips.

Innovation seeking
Looking through recent innovation in other industries shows that generally there is an increase in the use of plastics. In fastening a plastic catch has been recently introduced for holding thin sheets of metal together during fabrication. These take two forms, shown below, and may be adaptable for use as a paper clip.

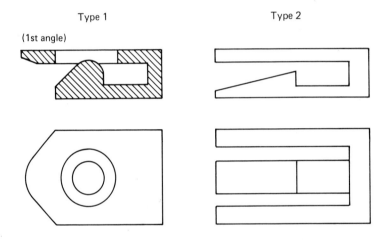

Type 1   Type 2

(1st angle)

Also a prefinished plastic coated rod is used in the furniture industry and this may be obtainable in narrow wire gauge.

Question: Does the design project still meet the management requirements?

1. The pricing and demand anticipated in the status specification is unchanged from that identified in the product definition.
2. The tooling cost for the familiar design is anticipated at a maximum cost of £30000 (and this is expected to be the major development cost) and total design and development costs inside the allowed £99000 for the lower production requirement of 50 million paper clips.
3. The tooling can be available for production for the familiar design in about five months from the go-ahead. We could therefore be in production within the year.

Answer: Yes.

Question: Is the approximate price and demand still right for your production equipment?

3 April 1989: Memo to Market Research Manager, Sales Manager and Design Manager, from Production Manager
The status specification does not alter the apparent viability of the paper clip from the production point of view for the familiar wire design. If either of the plastic clips is shown to be a better prospect, after the product status questionnaires have been answered, a different situation will exist.

A quick look at the price of injection moulding machines and their operating costs suggests that the cost of a suitable machine to produce a plastic clip would be £35 000 and two such machines would be needed to achieve the annual output of 50 million paper clips. The tooling would be subcontracted but would cost only £20 000 for each machine and last for 100 million clips. The delivery of the tooling would be four months as would the machines, so we could still meet the production start-up by the end of the year.

A rough cost breakdown is shown below:

Set-up costs for 50 million paper clips:
2 machines at £35 000	=	£70 000
2 sets of tooling at £20 000	=	£40 000
		£110 000

Maximum development cost allowed £99 000
Plastic clip not viable

50 million:
Unit material cost	=	0.150p
Unit machining cost*	=	0.107p
Unit tooling cost	=	0.020p
Manufacturing cost		0.277p

*7500 clips/hour

Running cost £8/hour
Manufacturing cost too high

Set-up costs for 100 million paper clips:
4 machines at	£35 000	= £140 000
4 sets of tooling at £20 000	=	£80 000
		£220 000

Maximum development costs allowed £150 000
Plastic clip not viable

It is hoped the status questionnaires will not show that the familiar metal paper clip design is conceptually vulnerable.

Answer: Yes for the familiar metal paper clip, No for the new plastic design.

Question: Is the approximate price and demand still right for sales and distribution?

3 April 1989: Memo to Sales Manager, Market Research Manager, Production Manager and Design Manager from Distribution and Transport Manager
At this stage the cost of sales and distribution appear viable for the project and can be made available without significant investment. Whatever the design of clip, the method of distribution appears to be the same and, therefore, I have looked more thoroughly into the costs of distribution and believe that these can be reduced to £230 for a delivery of one million or £400 for a delivery of two million by some rescheduling of work routes and lorries. Export, if reconsidered, would be £1000 for a delivery of two million paper clips.

Answer: Yes.

Questionnaire A Macro: Starting a new product design

Product type under consideration: **Plastic paper clips**

Comparison with which product: **Familiar metal paper clip**

	Yes (static)	No (dynamic)
1. If there has not been any technical advance recently that may be used to replace this product, tick the 'Yes' column and go on to Question 6. If there has, name it and tick the 'No' column.		Plastic ✓ paper clip
2. Is there a large infrastructure based on the existing design that *cannot* be used with the new design (e.g. fuel, sales, spares, distribution, servicing, skills etc.)? Give one tick in the 'Yes' column for each, or one tick in the 'No' column if there are none.		✓
3. Are there any conformance standards for this product that cannot be met by the new design?		✓
4. Put a tick in the 'No' column for every *two* advantages of the technical advance that would make a customer change from the existing product (one tick for lower price). (Think ahead. Could investment in the manufacturing process make the technical advance cheaper than the current product?)		Longer ✓ shelf life Better appearance
5. Put one tick in the 'Yes' column for every *two* disadvantages that would make a customer prefer the existing product.	Higher price Weaker 1½ Larger ✓	
6. Are a few relatively large companies dominating this product market? Tick the 'No' column if any technical advance mentioned in Question 1 comes from one of these companies.	✓	
7. Do most companies making this product appear to to copy each other?	✓	
8. Has the product been available in its present form for more than five years?	✓	
9. Tick the 'Yes' column if the number of your competitors is decreasing or remaining the same, tick the 'No' column if it has increased.	✓	
10. Recently there may have been changes in the economic climate, legislation or resources that make the existing product more (or less) viable to customers. Tick the 'Yes' column if these changes have made the existing product more viable or attractive to customers. Tick the 'No' column if these changes have made the existing product less viable or attractive to customers. (If neither, leave blank.)	—	—
Total:	5½	4

Judgement: **Plastic paper clip will not replace metal clip until price can be reduced.**

Questionnaire B Micro: New product or updating an existing product

Product name: **Paper clip**

	Yes (static)	No (dynamic)
1. Does this product interface with other products or fit an assembly not made by your company?	Paper ✓	
*2. Do you/will you use much dedicated machinery or automation in the manufacture of this product?	✓	
*3. Do you/will you use CAD for the design of this product?		✓
*4. Does your company have a greater market share or turnover than most of your competitors (or potential competitors)?	✓	
†5. Is a fast design time one of the three most important considerations when embarking on a new design?	✓ One year	
†6. Must new designs use the existing sales force and/or distribution networks?		✓
†7. Must new designs use the existing production facilities?	Financial ✓ constraints	
†8. Must tried and proven methods be used in the design of new products?	Financial ✓ constraints	
†9. Must new designs be an extension of the existing product range?		✓
10. Is this product made by assembling components the majority of which are made by other companies?	—	
11. Is more process design done than product design? (Design of the production method rather than of the product.)	—	
12. Has the product design specification remained significantly unaltered recently by your market research department and by your main customers?	—	
13. Do you use the same components from this product in several other products?	✓ Wire	
Total	7	3

*If a 'Yes' answer is given to these questions it is in your company's interest to seek static products. *To our advantage to seek static products.*

†'Yes' answers to these questions suggest that your company is restricting design to static design. Is this necessary or sensible? *Necessarily restricting design to static in Questions 11 and 12 to stay within financial constraints.*

Question: Do you still have the expertise, experience and technology needed for this market?
Answer: Yes for the wire paper clip, no for the plastic paper clip.

Question: Is it worth adapting the company?
Answer: Yes for the familiar metal paper clip, no for the plastic paper clip.

Second design review

Proceed to Layer 3: Ascertain product status

13 April 1989: Memo to Market Researcher, Sales Manager, Marketing Manager, Production Manager and Materials and Production Manager, from Design Manager
I have completed the Macro and Micro product status questionnaires, which are shown on the attached sheets. The metal paper clip, I am pleased to say, appears to be a static design which is not under any significant threat from any new plastic design, although the situation may change if the price of plastic falls significantly in relation to the cost of wire (which I will keep an eye on). There will be no design work undertaken on either plastic paper clip design.
   The Micro questionnaire suggests that this company is well suited for the production of a static design of this type and we should be able to compete effectively in the market.
   The original management requirements do not inhibit the design of this product.

Question: Could you answer the two questionnaires with confidence?
Answer: Yes.

Question: Is your design proposal conceptually vulnerable?
Answer: No.

Question: Is there a status mismatch between your company and the proposed product?
Answer: No.

Third design review

Proceed to Layer 4

Layer 4A: Write the product design specification
This is a lengthy and thorough document compiled by all interested parties and it has not been included here, as many pages would be required and not all the information is available.

Grade the elements of specification for importance

4 May 1989: Memo to Design Manager, Sales Manager and Designers, from Market Researcher
Our recent study of paper clip users suggests the following order for the most important features of a paper clip:

1. Sufficient strength to hold the paper.
2. Low purchase price.
3. Ease of taking off and putting on the paper.
4. Lightness.
5. Corrosion resistance. This is similar to long shelf life as paper clips are often purchased in large quantities and left on documents for several years. Corrosion over time leaves marks on the paper.

Other features were considered of less importance, although warehouses require a regular weekly delivery which must be reliable.

Current users felt that the familiar design already exhibited the features listed in 1, 4 and 5. A range of paper clip sizes and colours was given little importance by customers.

Product disposal

5 May 1989: Memo to Design Manager, from Market Research Manager
I have been investigating any problem that might be considered under the broad heading of 'product disposal'. The quantity of material used in a paper clip does not warrant the cost of any reclamation of damaged paper clips for recycling. The materials used are not toxic or hazardous and the product has a long shelf life before degradation. There will certainly be no market for servicing or spares and therefore we need not consider service centres or the necessary training of personnel. It would appear that, as a product, the paper clip can be forgotten once it has been delivered to our distributors.

Layer 4B: Relate design disciplines to the product status

5 May 1989: Memo to Designers, Material and Production Engineer, Quality Engineer, Test Engineer, Tool Room Manager and Purchasing Manager, from Design Manager
As the design appears to be static we will be concentrating our design effort on the improvement of the familiar design and its method of manufacture, bearing in mind the important design elements as identified by the market researcher.

We can disregard the disciplines associated with a dynamic design and below I have listed the disciplines associated with Static 1 design which perhaps we should consider in depth.

1. Imitation – copy the familiar design.
2. Use of standards – none.
3. Maintainability – not required.
4. Ergonomics* – can we make the paper clip easier to use? Look into ease of putting on and taking off the paper.
5. Aesthetics – can we improve the product appearance? How about the prefinished plastic coated wire identified in Layer 2?
6. CAD – we do not have this and the simplicity of the design does not justify it, but what about for the tooling? Do we produce enough similar tools for our product to justify CAD?
7. Size reduction – the standard size of paper clip commands 90 per cent of demand (Layer 2: Competition analysis) so we cannot alter this, but can we produce the same basic size using less than 10 cm of wire increasing lightness* but retaining strength?*
8. Low-cost production* – we will be using dedicated machinery. (See Layer 5: this is most important.)
9. Finish – the paper clip must not scratch the paper (Layer 2).
10. Effective purchasing* – the material cost is 52 per cent of the total manufacturing cost and therefore any savings in material purchase price would be reflected directly in profits.
11. Assembly aids – no assembly needed.
12. Group technology – not relevant.
13. Reduction of scrap – for each 1 per cent of production lost through scrap we lose 4 per cent loss in manufacturing profit (see Static 2).
14. Cost reduction* – if any other savings can be made in the product or process design or administration and handling please inform me as these can further improve profitability.

*These were identified as being the important elements, or contributing to these important elements, by market research.

5 May 1989: Memo to Sales Manager from Design Manager
Being a static design, the following features of marketing mix are important in the early stages of production.

1. Business planning – you can plan your strategy some way into the future in the knowledge that the product design will not change significantly over a foreseeable period (for example, planned market penetration).
2. Fast delivery – the initial requirements of deliveries weekly will be met as outlined in Layer 1.
3. Good reputation with customers – this is considered important to gain an edge over the competition making a very similar product.
4. After-sales service – not required.
5. Distribution system – a static design allows you to plan the distribution system with some consistency and, knowing that the distribution system will remain constant, you can seek the most efficient rates.
6. Advertising, promotion, credit policy.

19 May 1989: Memo to Design Manager, from Designers
We have considered the design of the paper clip and can make some improvements in the features you suggested.

1. Ergonomics – we can angle the tooling to give a better opening for sliding the paper into the clip, as shown below:

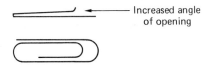

2. Aesthetics – the purchasing manager has found that the cost of coloured plastic-coated wire is twice that of standard nickel-coated wire and therefore we cannot improve the aesthetics viably.
3. CAD – we are currently investigating the supply of CAD equipment and the possible time savings in our annual tool design requirements.
4. Size reduction – by squaring some of the corners and reducing overlap of the wire we have been able to save ½ cm of material on each clip. The test engineer has found only 2 per cent loss in strength, which is acceptable.
5. Finish – we can stretch as we crop the wire. This avoids burrs which can damage the paper and adds 2 per cent to the cost of tooling (£600), i.e. 0.0006p/clip, which is viable.
6. Effective purchasing – the purchasing manager can order material on a three-year contract with fortnightly call-off, which is possible as the clip is a static design, and this will save 0.01p/per clip on the original size.
7. Reduction of scrap – we will be confronting this in Layer 5.

Latest production costs
Material cost 0.090 – 5% (size reduction) = 0.0855p
Unit machining cost unchanged   = 0.0670p
Unit tooling cost 0.02 + 2%   = 0.0306p
   (Layer 2 £30 000)
                                        ‾‾‾‾‾‾‾‾
Total manufacturing cost   = 0.1831p

These new figures may make a larger market viable.

Iteration

19 June 1989: Memo to Design Manager, Sales Manager and Production Manager, from Marketing Manager

In view of the latest manufacturing costs we have determined the market size more closely and anticipate that for a selling price of 0.3p/clip we could secure a home market of 72 million paper clips/year and an export market of 10 million.

22 June 1989: Memo to Design Manager, from Purchasing Manager
The cost of material for this latest market option on the same purchasing contract as before works out at 0.07p/clip based on the latest length of wire needed/clip.

22 June 1987: Memo to Design Manager, from Transport and Distribution Manager
The cost of distribution for this latest market option works out at 0.021p/paper clip in the UK. The export distribution costs are unchanged.

25 June 1989: Memo to Export Sales Coordinator, from Design Manager
Export of the paper clip now appears possible on quantities of 10 million/year. Please advise any international requirements you would like to be considered in the product design specification.

(A) *50 million option*

Latest manufacturing cost	= 0.1831p
Latest distribution cost	= 0.023p
Selling price = 0.33p	− 0.2061p = 0.1269p
Profit/clip = 0.1269p	
Profit on 50m production	= £63450

(B) *80 million UK option*

Material cost = 0.070 − 5%	= 0.0665p
Machining	= 0.0670p
Tooling	= 0.0306p
Total manufacturing cost	= 0.1641p
Manufacturing cost	= 0.1641p
Distribution UK	= 0.02p
Selling price = 0.25p	− 0.1841p = 0.0659p
Profit/clip = 0.0659p	
Profit on 80m production	= £52720

+20 million export

Manufacturing cost	= 0.1641p
Export distribution	= 0.050p
Selling price = 0.25p	− 0.2141p = 0.0359p
Profit/clip = 0.0359p	
Profit on 20 million production =	£7180
Total profit on option B	= £52720
	£59900 (less than option A)

(C) *72 million UK option*

Material cost	= 0.0700p
Machining	= 0.0670p
Tooling	= 0.0306p
Total manufacturing cost	= 0.1676p

Manufacturing cost   = 0.1676p
Distribution UK   = 0.0210p
Selling price = 0.3p   − 0.1886p = 0.1114p

Profit/clip = 0.1114p
Profit on 72 million production =   £80 208

+10 million export:
Manufacturing cost   = 0.1676p
Export distribution   = 0.050p
Selling price = 0.300p   − 0.2176p = 0.0824p

Profit/clip = 0.0824p
Profit on 10 million production =   £8 240
Total profit on option C   = £80 208
                                  ─────────
                                    £88 448

On a production of 82 million × 0.3p
Turnover = £246 000 (exceeds management requirement)
Gross margin = 36% (exceeds management requirements).

Fourth design review

Proceed to Layer 5: Static 2

25 May 1989: Memo to Designer (Jig and Tool), Material and Production Engineer, Quality Manager and Tool Room Manager, from Design Manager
The production volume allows immediate consideration of the disciplines associated with Static 2. The following should be considered in your process design.

1. Rationalization − the company will be concentrating on the manufacture of one size of paper clip made from wire it uses in other products.
2. Specialization − the company is already correctly structured from its previous experience with mass production.
3. Value analysis − if the design has been correctly undertaken in Static 1 this should not be possible now, but may be valid in some years when technology or prices change.
4. Very low-cost production
5. Dedicated machinery   } The process design must incorporate all these, and will
6. Automation   } need to, to reach the production volume and price.
7. Economies of scale
8. Long production runs − the static design will enable us to design the process equipment for long; uninterrupted production runs, use long-life tooling.
9. Computer control of production − this may be viable and will be considered after the costs of design and development have been recovered in eighteen months' time, as the price of the necessary technology is expected to fall.
10. Energy conservation in product use − not applicable.
11. Add-on product features − not applicable.
12. Energy conservation in production − match the power needed to operate the production process closely to the machine's driving-power requirements. Can we utilize cheap-rate electricity?
13. Volume maximization − in view of your cost reduction through the design of the paper clip using the disciplines of Static 1 we may be able to increase the production volume

and, using marginal productivity, we expect to be maximizing volume to lower the effect of fixed costs.

14. Elimination of scrap – the very high production volume means that almost any percentage of scrap will result in a high loss of revenue (e.g. 2 per cent scrap on the 50 million output = £1831 direct loss or £3300 loss of potential sales) as well as other problems, such as difficulty in meeting delivery dates, shorter than expected useful tool life and having a poor reputation with customers. It is therefore worth, with these high volumes, spending some extra time now to ensure the production process avoids scrap.

The company already has the capability to achieve many of these, which is why a high-volume static product is suitable for us (Micro questionnaire).

25 May 1989: Memo to Sales Manager, from Design Manager
A high-volume static design enables you to consider the following features of marketing mix.

1. Maximize market share – we will not be at full production capacity and production costs will continue to fall, the more we can produce. To gain an advantage over our competitors manufacturing the same product and using the same technology it is necessary that we achieve a substantial market share as quickly as possible.
2. Use of familiarity of product – most people recognize a paper clip and will attempt to purchase the familiar design when they need it. Perhaps you can use this feature to sell the product. A known effective design at a lower price?
3. Cost reduction in distribution and selling – just as production costs fall with higher volumes it may be possible to lower the unit cost of distribution and selling. With assured quantity deliveries for the foreseeable future it is worth attempting to seek out lower costs in this and in your method of selling.

26 May 1989: Memo to Production Manager, from Purchasing Manager

Kanban
I have contacted our material suppliers and requested that they should deliver our wire supply for use on the paper clips every 2 working days. They have answered, stating that our material demand does not warrant such frequent deliveries. They are only prepared to deliver as already stated, every fortnight. We will therefore need to retain the space allocated for storing the wire rolls in the warehouse.

27 May 1989: Memo to Design Manager from Jig and Tool Designer
Process design patents
Further to my memo of the 19th. The wire cropping tool appears to be a novel design. Should we attempt to patent or register this process design?

25 June 1989: Memo to Design Manager, from Designer
The manufacture and tooling of the paper clip have been considered and we can incorporate all the requirements of Static 2 disciplines.

We will be using dedicated machinery with fully automated material feed operating at the speeds described in Layer 1. We can use cheap-rate electricity during the evening shift and the machine used delivers 10 per cent more power than we require, which is the nearest we can achieve using the currently underutilized machinery.

We have spent some time on the question of scrap elimination and are now certain that our tooling design and manufacturing process can ensure this.

Production tooling and testing will be complete, as stated in Layer 1, in five months – 26 November 1989.

3 December 1989: Memo to Board of Directors, from Design Manager
We have completed the design of the paper clip and it is now in production one month ahead of schedule. With the knowledge that the design of the paper clip is static we have concentrated our effort on the disciplines associated with static design and the production volume warranted us also including the disciplines from Static 2. Through following these disciplines we have been able to design the paper clip to reach a larger market than we originally anticipated and can also compete in the export market.

Both turnover and gross margin are expected to exceed the requirements you put down and the total cost of design and development (including tooling) has been £120000, which will be repaid in eighteen months at the expected production rate.

Design circle

After the preliminary layer of the design process the first design circle will be assembled to undertake the tasks of Layer 1. The Design Manager, in this example, has been chosen to coordinate the design process and he will be a member of the design circle throughout, even though other people may join and leave as the design progresses. The typical make-up of the design circle will be as follows.

Preliminary Layer – Directors

Layer 1: *Product definition*
1. Design Manager
2. Marketing Manager
3. Production Manager
4. Sales Manager
5. Purchasing Manager
6. Accountant
7. Export Sales Coordinator

Design review

Layer 2: *Status specification*
1. Design Manager
2. Marketing Manager
3. Production Manager
4. Distribution and Transport Manager
5. Tool Room Manager
6. Designer
7. Market Researcher
8. Test Engineer
9. Purchasing Manager

Design review

Layer 3: *Ascertain the product status*
1. Design Manager
2. Marketing Manager
3. Market Researcher
4. Designer
5. Materials and Production Engineer

Design review

Layer 4A

Write the product design specification

Two design circles needed, both coordinated by the Design Manager:

Design circle A	Design circle B
1. Design Manager	1. Design Manager
2. Market Research Manager	2. Material and Production Engineer
3. Sales Manager	3. Production Manager
4. Distribution and Transport Manager	4. Test Engineer
5. Designer	5. Purchasing Manager
6. Market Researcher	6. Quality Engineer
7. Export Sales Coordinator	7. Designer

Grade the elements of the specification for importance
1. Design Manager
2. Market Researcher
3. Designer (Jig and Tool)
4. Designer

Design review

Layer 4B: *Relate design disciplines to the product status*
1. Design Manager
2. Designer
3. Designer
4. Materials and Production Engineer
5. Tool Room Manager
6. Purchasing Manager
7. Quality Engineer
8. Test Engineer

Concept design: Design review

Detail design: Design review

Layer 5
1. Design Manager
2. Designer (Jig and Tool)
3. Tool Room Manager
4. Purchasing Manager
5. Materials and Production Engineer
6. Production Manager
7. Quality Engineer
8. Test Engineer
9. Sales Manager

Quality circle
1. Design Manager
2. Designer (Jig and Tool)
3. Quality Engineer
4. Materials and Production Engineer
5. Production Operatives (Designer, Purchasing Manager, Tool Room Manager and Test Engineer when necessary)

A design review should follow each stage of design. It can be seen that at the start of design those involved in the process have a more senior function, the preliminary layer being undertaken by the board of directors. The design is then taken through the various layers of the design process under the constant direction of the Design Manager. Seniority is reduced and authority delegated, the further the design proceeds. In this example the possibility of export is eliminated early on and the Export Sales Coordinator takes no further part in the design until Layer 4, when an export market again seems possible. All departments are involved during some part of the design.

At Layer 4A the product design specification is written and in this case 13 people will be involved. The design circle will only operate effectively with nine people or fewer and therefore at this stage two design circles will operate in parallel, both under the management of and *coordinated by* the Design Manager. The people involved in Circles A and B have been identified. In this case, Circle B is more involved with the production side of the paper clip. Operating two circles should be avoided if possible, but not to the elimination of anyone who may have a useful contribution to make towards providing the optimum solution to any design element.

At the concept design stage the static product status suggests that seeking a new concept for the product is unnecessary, but seeking a new concept for the production tooling may be worthwhile. After the design review the detail design of both the product and process are considered. The design disciplines of Static 1 will guide the design and indicate who should be involved in the design circle at this stage.

In most designs, manufacture and sales will begin at this point and consideration of the disciplines with Static 2 need only start when the production volume has built up. With the paper clip the product only becomes viable with a very high volume of production, and therefore the disciplines associated with Static 2 should be confronted before production. Design effort at this stage is very heavily production orientated and the design circle personnel reflect this.

Manufacture and selling of the paper clip will then start and the design circle will meet periodically to review the progress of the product and to solve any problems or propose further cost reductions or design improvements. These subsequent meetings will take the form more usually associated with quality circles, which are, in effect, process design circles.

With some products the design circle will need to reconvene to implement the disposal plans of the product. These may cover aspects of the products' service requirements and reclamation of re-usable of hazardous or toxic waste. The plans for disposal will have been fully itemized in the original PDS and therefore the design circle will only need to act out these plans and recommendations.

In this hypothetical example the design process has been well structured and organized. The result was a potentially successful product on the market.

8 An example of the need for the product definition

The Sinclair C5 was defined, produced and marketed as an electric car. The questionnaires below compare the product as a technical advance trying to enter three markets: cars, mopeds and bicycles. The first questionnaire shows that the C5 was certainly unlikely to affect the static plateau of the car market and the second also indicates that it was unable to compete with a moped, although the advantages and disadvantages change significantly. For example, the C5 was less comfortable than a car but more comfortable than a moped, It had worse weather protection than a car but the same weather protection as a moped.

When the C5 is compared with a bicycle the comparison is much closer, which suggests that if the C5 had been produced and marketed as a bicycle (especially as a bicycle for the unfit) or for senior citizens (but not for the disabled) it might have taken a share of the bicycle market.

Had Sinclair started out on the project having defined the C5 as a bicycle for the elderly they could have organized production quantities suited to that market. Marketing and advertising would also have been aimed at this much smaller market and expenditure contained to generate a profit within it. Alternatively, it could have been decided that this market was likely to be too small to generate sufficient profits and the entire project would not have been started.

The questionnaire also suggests that, even as a bicycle for senior citizens, the C5 required more advantages over a bicycle to make it a serious competitor, and this could have helped to direct design emphasis later in the design process. For example, including better weather protection and load-carrying (shopping) capacity might have given it an edge in that market.

It can be seen that product definition is of prime importance for directing the subsequent design process and has a great effect on the success in the market of the final product.

A further interesting dimension of the questionnaire is that it shows that the electric car can never end the static plateau of the current internal combustion engine until a new battery 'breakthrough' is made which can significantly increase the speed and range of the car. After twenty years of work and government aid over the past ten years, production of battery derivatives for vans has not made a significant impact on the market.

Questionnaire A Macro: Starting a new product design
Product type under consideration: **Sinclair C5**
Comparison with which product: **Car**

	Yes (static)	*No (dynamic)*
1. If there has not been any technical advance recently that may be used to replace this product, tick the 'Yes' column and go on to Question 6. If there has, name it and tick the 'No' column.		Sinclair ✓ C5
2. Is there a large infrastructure based on the existing design that *cannot* be used with the new design (e.g. fuel, sales, spares, distribution, servicing, skills etc.)? Give one tick in the 'Yes' column for each, or one tick in the 'No' column if there are none.	Fuel ✓ Sales ✓	
3. Are there any conformance standards for this product that cannot be met by the new design?		✓
4. Put a tick in the 'No' column for every *two* advantages of the technical advance that would make a customer change from the existing product (one tick for lower price). (Think ahead. Could investment in the manufacturing process make the technical advance cheaper than the current product?)	Question 5: Passenger space, storage space, Q+R, safer, faster, stronger, more range, larger, higher load, more comfortable, higher status, more add-on features, longer life, better weather protection = 7½ ✓	Question 4: Less pollution, more economical, easier to use, quieter, less legislation, lighter, less tax and insurance, easier maintenance, more convenient (parking, storing), lower price = 5½ ✓
5. Put one tick in the 'Yes' column for every *two* disadvantages that would make a customer prefer the existing product.		
6. Are a few relatively large companies dominating this product market? Tick the 'No' column if any technical advance mentioned in Question 1 comes from one of these companies.	✓	
7. Do most companies making this product appear to to copy each other?	✓	
8. Has the product been available in its present form for more than five years?	✓	
9. Tick the 'Yes' column if the number of your competitors is decreasing or remaining the same. Tick the 'No' column if it has increased.	Fewer car manufacturers ✓	
10. Recently there may have been changes in the economic climate, legislation or resources that make the existing product more (or less) viable to customers. Tick the 'Yes' column if these changes have made the existing product more viable or attractive to customers. Tick the 'No' column if these changes have made the existing product less viable or attractive to customers. (If neither, leave blank.)		
Total:	13½	7½

Judgement: **The Sinclair C5 will not compete with a car.**

Questionnaire A Macro: Starting a new product design
Product type under consideration: **Sinclair C5**
Comparison with which product: **Moped**

	Yes (static)	No (dynamic)
1. If there has not been any technical advance recently that may be used to replace this product, tick the 'Yes' column and go on to Question 6. If there has, name it and tick the 'No' column.		Sinclair ✓ C5
2. Is there a large infrastructure based on the existing design that *cannot* be used with the new design (e.g. fuel, sales, spares, distribution, servicing, skills etc.)? Give one tick in the 'Yes' column for each, or one tick in the 'No' column if there are none.	Fuel ✓	
3. Are there any conformance standards for this product that cannot be met by the new design?		✓
4. Put a tick in the 'No' column for every *two* advantages of the technical advance that would make a customer change from the existing product (one tick for lower price). (Think ahead. Could investment in the manufacturing process make the technical advance cheaper than the current product?)	Question 5: Passenger space, Q+R, safer, stronger, faster, more range, higher load, more eco-nomical, higher status, longer life in use, more convenient (parking, stor-ing) = 5½ ✓	Question 4: Stability, main-tainability, easier to use, quieter, less pol-lution, more comfortable, less legislation (crash helmet), less tax and insurance = 4 ✓
5. Put one tick in the 'Yes' column for every *two* disadvantages that would make a customer prefer the existing product.		
6. Are a few relatively large companies dominating this product market? Tick the 'No' column if any technical advance mentioned in Question 1 comes from one of these companies.	✓	
7. Do most companies making this product appear to to copy each other?	✓	
8. Has the product been available in its present form for more than five years?	✓	
9. Tick the 'Yes' column if the number of your competitors is decreasing or remaining the same. Tick the 'No' column if it has increased.	✓	
10. Recently there may have been changes in the economic climate, legislation or resources that make the existing product more (or less) viable to customers. Tick the 'Yes' column if these changes have made the existing product more viable or attractive to customers. Tick the 'No' column if these changes have made the existing product less viable or attractive to customers. (If neither, leave blank.)		✓ Legislation on user age and moped speed
Total:	10½	7

Judgement: **The moped will not be replaced by the Sinclair C5.**

Questionnaire A Macro: Starting a new product design
Product type under consideration: **Sinclair C5**
Comparison with which product: **Bicycle (used by an unfit, not disabled, person)**

	Yes (static)	No (dynamic)
1. If there has not been any technical advance recently that may be used to replace this product, tick the 'Yes' column and go on to Question 6. If there has, name it and tick the 'No' column.		Sinclair C5 ✓
2. Is there a large infrastructure based on the existing design that *cannot* be used with the new design (e.g. fuel, sales, spares, distribution, servicing, skills etc.)? Give one tick in the 'Yes' column for each, or one tick in the 'No' column if there are none.		✓
3. Are there any conformance standards for this product that cannot be met by the new design?		✓
4. Put a tick in the 'No' column for every *two* advantages of the technical advance that would make a customer change from the existing product (one tick for lower price). (Think ahead. Could investment in the manufacturing process make the technical advance cheaper than the current product?)		Stability, easier to use, faster, more range, more comfortable, higher status, no physical effort = 3½ ✓
5. Put one tick in the 'Yes' column for every *two* disadvantages that would make a customer prefer the existing product.	Q+R, less maintenance, lower price, lower running cost, longer life in use, more convenient (parking, storing) = 3½ ✓	
6. Are a few relatively large companies dominating this product market? Tick the 'No' column if any technical advance mentioned in Question 1 comes from one of these companies.		✓
7. Do most companies making this product appear to copy each other?	✓	
8. Has the product been available in its present form for more than five years?	✓	
9. Tick the 'Yes' column if the number of your competitors is decreasing or remaining the same. Tick the 'No' column if it has increased.	✓	
10. Recently there may have been changes in the economic climate, legislation or resources that make the existing product more (or less) viable to customers. Tick the 'Yes' column if these changes have made the existing product more viable or attractive to customers. Tick the 'No' column if these changes have made the existing product less viable or attractive to customers. (If neither, leave blank.)	—	—
Total:	6½	7½

Judgement: **The Sinclair C5 has a better chance of a niche in this than in other markets.**

Questionnaire A Macro: Starting a new product design
Product type under consideration: **Electric battery van derivative**
Comparison with which product: **Petrol van**

	Yes (static)	No (dynamic)
1. If there has not been any technical advance recently that may be used to replace this product, tick the 'Yes' column and go on to Question 6. If there has, name it and tick the 'No' column.	✓ Not recently	
2. Is there a large infrastructure based on the existing design that *cannot* be used with the new design (e.g. fuel, sales, spares, distribution, servicing, skills etc.)? Give one tick in the 'Yes' column for each, or one tick in the 'No' column if there are none.	Fuel ✓ Servicing ✓	
3. Are there any conformance standards for this product that cannot be met by the new design?		✓
4. Put a tick in the 'No' column for every *two* advantages of the technical advance that would make a customer change from the existing product (one tick for lower price). (Think ahead. Could investment in the manufacturing process make the technical advance cheaper than the current product?)		Cheaper to insure, easier maintenance, easier to use, quieter, less pollution = 2½ ✓
5. Put one tick in the 'Yes' column for every *two* disadvantages that would make a customer prefer the existing product.	Faster refuelling, lower price, faster, more range, higher load, more economical, larger or lighter = 3½ ✓	
6. Are a few relatively large companies dominating this product market? Tick the 'No' column if any technical advance mentioned in Question 1 comes from one of these companies.	✓	
7. Do most companies making this product appear to to copy each other?	✓	
8. Has the product been available in its present form for more than five years?	✓	
9. Tick the 'Yes' column if the number of your competitors is decreasing or remaining the same. Tick the 'No' column if it has increased.	✓	
·10. Recently there may have been changes in the economic climate, legislation or resources that make the existing product more (or less) viable to customers. Tick the 'Yes' column if these changes have made the existing product more viable or attractive to customers. Tick the 'No' column if these changes have made the existing product less viable or attractive to customers. (If neither, leave blank.)	✓ Lower oil prices	
Total:	11½	3½

Judgement: **At present the electric van is not a threat to the petrol van.**

Appendix   The research that led to this book

The research that underpins this book was started in February 1985. It was decided to investigate the design of particular products and, having selected the products, wherever possible, all the manufacturers servicing the British market were visited in order to ascertain their design practices. The visit took the form of a structured interview based on a questionnaire and this was given to the most senior person responsible for, and having an input into, the design of the particular product under investigation. The questionnaire was formulated to investigate certain hypotheses which, it was believed, could improve the organization of the product design process. Following each interview, the results were analysed and compared to the original hypotheses and a report sent to the company concerned describing the findings and making suggestions as to how the company might improve its design management. This was accompanied by a feedback questionnaire which gauged the interviewee's opinion on the accuracy and content of the report. Several subsequent contacts were made to discuss aspects of the report and the research. Feedback was almost all positive, stating that the report was an accurate interpretation of what had been said at the interview, was an accurate description of the company and the recommendations appeared to be useful.

The advantage of investigating particular products was that with background research the relative success and failure in the market could be gauged and it was possible to detect design leaders and innovators through various methods, such as parametric analysis, analysis of market size, company share and position in that market. The relative strengths and weaknesses of the product design could also be ascertained. The products chosen were those of which we had particular knowledge, having either worked in the industries or having access to the history of the product design. In this way it was possible to pitch the discussions at a much higher level than is often the case with academic research carried out in industry. For ease of data collection and analysis, products were also selected in which there was little import penetration and few manufacturers so that, in theory, all the manufacturers supplying that product could be interviewed. Also products that were believed to be static and dynamic designs were chosen to give balanced research results. All the products had to have a suitable design 'content' and industrial products were also used in the research, as it is believed that these are purchased mainly for rational reasons and are not as subject to fashion and other factors that could confuse the results obtained. This ensured that the design effects could be shown up more clearly.

The total results from all the companies interviewed were then analysed together and the hypotheses that were upheld were identified. Those interviewed were strongly in favour of a system that would highlight areas of greater importance and show them how to undertake the front end of design. Therefore it was decided to put the results in a form that could be a useful and usable method for actually undertaking the management of design in industry, and this was the improved design process.

Several interesting findings were made in the research. It was discovered that certain companies should concentrate on static products and others on dynamic ones, but some can specialize in static design using the designs of others, and this can be an effective successful policy and predetermined strategy. Appreciation of product status can enable a company to organize its management strategy for optimum efficiency, but design must be linked with efficient marketing (research and sales) and production: weakness in any of these areas will cause a product to fail. When a product is static the larger companies are more likely to be successful, but when it is dynamic the advantages of a company being large are diminished.

At any point in time some products designs are static and some are dynamic. The early recognition of the static plateau can, in some cases, enable a company to set standards that become the market norm. By effective total design it is possible for a company to create a static plateau. Similarly, one can identify the innovation necessary to cause a static product to become dynamic again.

Maximizing market share is linked with maximizing static design in order to be successful. It is possible to list in order the value, or importance, of elements in the product design specification for certain categories of products in certain markets.

Appreciation of the product status highlights the strengths and weaknesses in the product design group and other areas of the company operation such as marketing and production. The company structure provides a mantle in which design operates, and this determines what type of design is undertaken. Company personnel must seek and evaluate innovations to determine if a product is becoming dynamic again. Dynamic design benefits from and requires an organic structure. On the other hand, only some static disciplines benefit from and require a mechanistic structure.

The findings of the research had determined many important features necessary for the successful designs of products, but to make these usable it was necessary to show when and where (or where not) these should be brought into design. After investigating various forms, a 'layered' approach was found to be most effective and popular. In this the person responsible for design is led through various stages of design, completing one layer before proceeding to the next.

Having produced the improved process for total design in a usable form it was supplied to design managers who, up to that time, had not been involved in the research but were known to be actually working on the organization of the front end of design. After a suitable period these companies were visited and comments and criticism noted through the aid of a questionnaire. The criticisms were of a minor nature, involving small changes to clarify the system. There was no criticism as to the approach format or content, and the design process was well received (in some cases, enthusiastically), being described as usable and in advance of current practice. Companies asked to retain the design process after the investigation for their use and reference.

All the aims of the research have been fulfilled and the resulting design process is both usable and workable as well as effective, especially through the identification and use of product status.

References

Abbott, H. (1980, *Design and Product Safety* and *Safe Enough to Sell*. London: The Design Council.

Abernathy, W.J. (1978), *The Productivity Dilemma: Roadblock to Innovation in the Automobile Industry*, Baltimore, MD: Johns Hopkins University Press.

Abernathy, W.J. and Utterback, J.M. (1975), 'A dynamic model of process and product innovation', *Omega*, 639–656.

Abernathy, W.J. and Utterback, J.M. (1978), 'Patterns of industrial innovation', *Technology Review*, **80**, 41–47.

Abernathy, W.J. and Wayne, K. (1974), 'Limits of the learning curve', *Harvard Business Review*, September–October, 109.

Alexander, M. (1985), 'Creative marketing and innovative consumer product design–some case studies', *Design Studies*, **6**, No. 1, January, 41–50.

Andrews, B. (1975), *Creative Product Development*, Harlow: Longman.

Ansoff, H.I. (1982), Chapter 2 in *Understanding and Managing Social Change*, H.I. Ansoff, A. Bosman and P.M. Storm (eds), North Holland.

Ansoff, H.I. and Stewart, J.M. (1967), 'Strategies for a technology based business', *Harvard Business Review*, November/December.

Archer, B. (1986), 'Conference reports', *Design Studies, 7*, No. 2, April, 113.

Bass, L.W. (1969), 'The management of research and development', Proc. Conf. University of Strathclyde, April, pp. 10–14.

Belbin, R.M. (1981), *Management Teams: Why They Succeed and Fail*, London: Heinemann.

Blois, K.J. and Cowell, D.W. (1973), *Short Cases in Marketing Management*, Glasgow: International Textbook Co. Ltd.

Booz Allen and Hamilton Inc. (1965, 1968), *The Management of New Products*, New York.

Booz Allen and Hamilton Inc. (1982), *New Products Management for the 1980's*, New York.

Bright, J.R. (1968), 'Some management lessons from technological innovation research', National Conference on Management of Technological Innovation. University of Bradford Management Centre.

Brown, D.C. and Chandrasekaran, B. (1983), 'An approach to expert systems for mechanical design', Proc. Trends and Applications 1983, National Bureau of Standards, Gaithersburg, MD, May.

BS 4778 (1979), Glossary of Terms Used in Quality Assurance, London: British Standards Institute.

Buggie, F.D. (1981), *New Product Development Strategies*, New York: Amacom, 27–28.

Burns, T. and Stalker, G.M. (1961), *The Management of Innovation*, London: Tavistock.

Carpenter, R.E., Kinnard, J., Van Mullen, F. and Wright, P. (1986), 'Product – market decisions: dancing on the razor's edge', *Planning Review*, 26.

Centre for the Study of Industrial Innovation (1971), 'On the shelf: a survey of industrial R&D projects abandoned for non-technical reasons', July, London.

Clausing, D.P. (1986), 'Competitiveness in manufacturing: design optimization', *Laboratory Newsletter, University of Missouri – Columbia*, **3**, No. 1, Spring.

Cooper, R.G. (1976), *Introducing Successful New Industrial Products*, MCB Monograms.

161

Cooper, R.G. (1983), 'A process model for industrial new product development', *IEEE Transactions of Engineering Management,* **EM30**, No. 1, February, 2–11.

Cooper, R.G. (1984), 'The impact of new product strategies', *Industrial Marketing Management*, 12.

Corfield, K.G. (Chairman) (1979), *Product Design*, London: National Economic Development Council, March.

Cowell, D.W. (1984), *The Marketing of Services*, London: Heinemann.

Deasley, P. (1986), 'Products – a strategic issue', *Engineering*, September, 604.

Design Council (1985), *Innovation. A Study of the Problems and Benefits of Product Innovation*, London.

Dixon, J.R. and Simmons, M.K. (1983), 'Computers that design: expert systems for mechanical engineers', *Computers in Mechanical Engineering*, November.

Dowdy, W.L and Nickolchev, J. (1986), 'Can industries de-mature? Applying new technologies to mature industries', *Long Range Planning*, **19**, No. 2, April, 38–49.

Doyle, P. (1976) 'The realities of the product life cycle', *Quarterly Review of Marketing*, Summer, 1–6.

Doyle, P., Saunders, J. and Wong, V. (1985), 'Why Japan outmarkets Britain', *Management Today*, May.

Drucker, P.F. (1974) *Management: Tasks, Responsibilities, Practices*, New York: Harper and Row.

Edosomwan, J.A. (1987), 'Ten design rules for knowledge based expert systems', *Industrial Engineering*, **19**, No. 8, August, 78–80.

Ehrlenspiel, K. (1984), 'Denkmodell Des Konstruktionsprozesses', *Schweizer Maschinemarkt*, No. 51 (Design Methodology: Strategy (39), Model of the Design Process).

Ellas, A.L. (1983), 'Computer-aided engineering: the A.I. connection', *American Institute of Aeronautics and Astronautics*, July–August, 48–54.

Fayol, H. (1971 [1949]), *General and Industrial Management*, translated from the French by B.C. Storrs, London: Pitman.

Feilden, G.B.R. *et al.* (1963), *Engineering Design (The Feilden Report)*, Dept of Scientific and Industrial Research, London: HMSO.

Foster, R. (1986), *Innovation, The Attacker's Advantage*, London: Macmillan.

Foxall, G.R. (1984), *Corporate Innovation: Marketing and Strategy*, London: Croom Helm.

Fullan, M. (1970), 'Industrial technology and worker integration in the organization', *American Sociological Review*, **35**, 1028–1039.

Gilbreth, F.B. and Gilbreth, L.M. (1973 [1916]), *Fatigue Study: The Elimination of Humanity's Greatest Unnecessary Waste: A First Step in Motion Study*, Easton, PA: Hive.

Gregory, S. (1966) *The Design Method*, London: Butterworths.

Gregory, S. (1985), 'Strategy and design', in *Design and Innovation*, edited by R. Langdon and R. Rothwell, London: Frances Pinter.

Hales, C. (1987), *Analysis of the Engineering Design Problems in an Industrial Context*, Cambridge: Gants Hill.

Hayes, R.H. and Abernathy, W.J. (1980), 'Managing our way to economic decline', *Harvard Business Review*, No. 58, July/August, 67–77.

Heller, R. (1984), *The Naked Market, Monitoring Methods for the 80s*, London: Sidgwick and Jackson.

Herriot, P. (1985), *Down From the Ivory Tower*, New York: Wiley, 44–45.

Herzberg, F., Mausner, B.S. and Snyderman, G. (1959), *The Motivation to Work*, New York: Wiley.

Hirsch, S. (1965), 'United States electronics industry in international trade', *National Institute Economic Review*, No. 34, November.

Hobbes, T. (1651), *The Leviathan*, edited by A.R. Waller, 1935.

Hollins, W.J. (1988), 'Product status and the management of design', *Engineering Design*, July.

Hollins, W.J. (1989), 'Innovation managed', *Eureka*, January–December (series of articles).

Huckerby, M. (1988), 'Justifiable act of faith', *Engineering Computers*, 28–29

Ingersol Engineers (1985), *News for Industry*, No. 7.

Institution of Production Engineers (1984), *A Guide to Design for Production*, London.

Johne, F.A. (1985), *Industrial Product Innovation: Organisation and Management*, London: Croom Helm.

Johne, F.A. and Snelson, P.A. (1988), 'Success factors in product innovation: a selective review of the literature', *Journal of Product Innovation Management*, **5**(2), 100–110.

Jones, J.C. (1970), *Design Methods: Seeds of Human Futures*, 2nd edn, Chichester: Wiley.

Kanter, R.M. (1983), *The Change Masters: Corporate Entrepreneurs at Work*, Counterpoint Allen and Unwin (1986): also titled *The Change Masters: Innovation for Productivity in the American Corporation*, New York: Simon and Schuster (1983).

Klein, B.H. (1977), *Dynamic Economics*, Cambridge, MA: Harvard University Press.

Kotler, P. (1985), *The New Competition*, Englewood Cliffs, NJ: Prentice-Hall.

Kuhn, T. (1962), *The Structure of Scientific Revolutions*, University of Chicago Press.

Lawrence, P.R. and Lorsch, J.W. (1967a), Differentiation and integration in complex organisations, *Administrative Science Quarterly*, No. 12, 1–47.

Lawrence, P.R. and Lorsch, J.W. (1967b), *Organisation and Environment: Managing Differentiation and Integration*, Cambridge, MA: Harvard University Press.

Levitt, T. (1960), 'Marketing myopia', *Harvard Business Review*, July/August.

Levitt, T. (1962), *Innovation in Marketing*, London: Pan.

Lock, D.L. (1968), *Project Management*, Aldershot: Gower.

Mansfield, E. (1968), *Economics of Technical Change*, New York: W.W. Norton.

Mansfield, E., Rapoport, J., Schnee, J., Wagner, S. and Hamburger, M. (1971), *Research and Innovation in the Modern Corporation*, New York: W.W. Norton.

Marquis, F. (1986), The Alvey Project, telephone conversation with the authors, 16 June.

Mayo, E. (1933), *The Human Problems of an Industrial Civilisation*, London: Macmillan.

McLeod, T.S. (1969), *Management of Research, Development and Design in Industry*, Aldershot: Gower, pp. 50–59.

Midgley, D.F. (1981), 'Toward a theory of the product life cycle: explaining diversity', *Journal of Marketing*, **45**, No. 3, 109–15.

Miller, R. and Sawyers, D. (1968), *The Technical Development of Modern Aviation*, London: Routledge.

Murrell, K.F.H. (1969), *Ergonomics*, London: Chapman & Hall.

Nelson, R. (1984), *High Technology Policies: A Five Nation Comparison*, Washington DC: American Enterprise Institute.

Nicholls, J.A.F. and Roslow, S. (1986), 'The "S-curve": an aid to strategic marketing', *The Journal of Consumer Marketing*, **3**, No. 2, Spring, 53.

Nyström, H. (1979), *Creativity and Innovation*, Chichester: Wiley.

Oakley, M. (1984), *Managing Product Design*, London: Weidenfeld and Nicolson.

O'Meara, J.T. Jnr (1961), 'Selecting profitable products', *Harvard Business Review*, January/February, 83.

Osborn, A. (1963), *Applied Imagination*, New York: Scribner.

O'Shaughnessy, J. (1984), *Competitive Marketing: A Strategic Approach*, London: Allen and Unwin.

Oxenfeldt, A.R. (1959), 'How to use market share measurement', *Harvard Business Review*, January/February, 66.

Parker, J.E.S. (1978), *The Economics of Innovation: The National and Multinational Enterprise in Technological Change*, 2nd edn, Harlow: Longman.

Parker, R.C. (1980), *Guidelines for Product Innovation*, London: BIM.

Parker, R.C. (1982), *The Management of Innovation*, Chichester: Wiley.

Parkinson, S.T. (1981), 'Successful new product development: an international comparative study', Conf. R & D Management, University of Strathclyde, 11 February.

Peters, T.J. and Waterman, R.H. (1982), *In Search of Excellence: Lessons from America's Best Run Companies*, New York: Harper and Row.

Pugh, S. (1981), *Design Decision–How to Succeed and Know Why*, Proc. Conf. Engineering Design, Birmingham, UK.

Pugh, S. (1982), *The Design Activity Model*, Engineering Design Centre, Loughborough University of Technology, June.

Pugh, S. (1983), 'The application of CAD in relation to dynamic/static product concepts', Conf. ICED83 Copenhagen, 15–18 August.

Pugh, S. (1984a), 'Further development of the hypothesis of static dynamic concepts in product design'. Proc. International Conf. Design and Synthesis, Tokyo, 216–221.

Pugh, S. (1984b), 'CAD/CAM – hindrance or help to design?' Proc. CFAO Conception et Fabrication Assistée par Ordinature, Université Libre De Bruxelles, October.

Pugh, S. (1985), *CAD/CAM–Its Effect on Design Understanding and Progress*, Proc. International Conf. CAD-CAM, Robotics and Automation, Tucson, AZ.

Pugh, S. (1989) 'Knowledge-based systems in the design activity', *Design Studies*, **10**, No. 4, 219–227.

Pugh, S. and Smith, D.G. (1976), 'CAD in the context of engineering design: the designer's viewpoint'. Proc. CAD 76, pp. 193–198.

Randall, G. (1980), 'Managing new products', *Management Survey Report No. 47*, London: BIM.

Rink, D.R. and Swan, J.E. (1979), 'Product life cycle research: a literature review', *Journal of Business Research*, **7**, No. 3, 219–242.

Rothwell, R. *et al.* (1972), *Factors for Success in Industrial Innovations, Project Sappho–A Comparative Study of Success and Failure in Industrial Innovations*, Sussex: Science Policy Research Unit.

Rothwell, R. (1977), 'The characteristics of successful innovators and technically progressive firms, **7**, No. 3, June: reprinted in *R & D Management Innovation: A Study of the Problems and Benefits of Product Innovation*, London: The Design Council, 1985.

Rothwell, R. (1985), 'Innovation policy: reindustrialisation and technology towards a national policy framework', *Science and Policy*, **12**, No. 3, June.

Rothwell, R. and Gardiner, P. (1984), 'Design and competition in engineering', *Long Range Planning*, **17**, No. 3, 79–91.

Rubenstein, A.H., Chakrabarti, A.K., O'Keefe, R.D., Souder, W.E., and Young, H.C. (1976), 'Factors influencing innovation success at the project level', *Research Management*, May, 15–20.

Schener, F.M. (1971), *Industrial Market Structure and Economic Performance*, Chicago, IL: Rand McNally.

Schoeffler, S., Buzzell, R.D. and Heany, D.F. (1974), 'Impact of strategic planning on profit performance', *Harvard Business Review*, **52**, March.

SEED (1985a), 'Curriculum for design engineering undergraduate course', Proc. of the Working Party for Discussion at SEED.

SEED (1985b), *Sharing Experience in Engineering Design*, 2nd Report. (Design Centre, School of Engineering, Hatfield Polytechnic, Hatfield, UK).

Shortliffe, E.H. (1976), *Computer based medical consultants: MYCIN*, American Elsevier.

Skinner, W. (1986), The Productivity Paradox, *Harvard Business Review*, July/August, p.53.

Starr, M.K. (1963), *Product Design and Decision Theory*, Englewood Cliffs, NJ: Prentice-Hall.

Stolte-Heiskanen, V. (1980),'A management view of research', *Science*, January, 9.

Taguchi, G. (1985), *Quality Engineering in Japan* (unpublished).

Takeuchi, H. and Nanaka, I. (1986), 'The new new product development game', *Harvard Business Review*, January/February, 137–146.

Taylor, F.W. (1911), *The Principles of Scientific Management*, New York: Harper, 1947.

Thackray, J. (1983), 'Troubled times for multinational business', *McKinsey Quarterly*, Summer.

Turner, B.T. (1983), 'Efficiency in the design office', Conf. Wembley, 15–16 June, Bury St Edmunds: Mechanical Engineering Publications.

Tushman, M. and Nadler, D. (1986), 'Organizing for innovation. Process innovation–cost and quality', *California Management Review*, **XXVIII**, No. 3, Spring, 74.

Twiss, B.C. (1980), *Managing Technological Innovation*, 2nd edn, Harlow: Longman.

Usher, A.P. (1929), *A History of Mechanical Inventions*, Boston, MA: Beacon Press.

Viewing, D. (1980), 'Product development strategy', The management of innovation–High technology innovation, Design Engineering Conference.

Wall, R.A. (ed.) (1986), *Finding and Using Product Information*, Aldershot: Gower.

Woodward, J. (1965), *Industrial Organisation: Theory and Practice*, Oxford: Oxford University Press.

Index

Aesthetics in design
  as dynamic discipline, 115
  and specification, 91
After-sales service, as design discipline, 117–118
Aircraft industry, and product status, 21
Automation, 126
  and product status, 31–32

British Standards
  5740 (Safeguarding Machinery), 28
  on quality/reliability, 92
  see also Standards

CAD/CAM, and product status, 19, 119
Calculators, and decline of slide rule, 22
Circles, see Design circles; Quality circles
Companies
  constraints, and design specification, 94
  failure, 'shake-out' during product
    development, 37
  size, and product status, 81–83
Competition analysis
  for design specification, 89–90
  and product status, 72, 73
Computer industry, microcomputers static
    plateau, 27
Costs
  of design, product status and, 66
  low-cost production and product status, 114
  and stage of design, 12–16
  of stockholding, 105
  target, in design specification, 89
  see also Financial control in design
Customers
  and design specification, 92
  resistance, and static plateau, 27–28
  selection by, and design, 9
  training, as dynamic design discipline, 113

Definition, see Product definition
Delivery, fast, as design discipline, 117
Design, see Total design process; Management of
    design
Design circles, 52–55
  for worked example, 150–152

Design specification, 84–107
  contents, 87–96
  element grading, 102–105
  features analysis in, 102
  guidelines for preparation, 96–97
  inadequacies, 86
  parametric analysis in, 98–102
  and product status, 29–30, 97
  worked example, 144–145
Diesel engine design effort, 28
Disposal considerations, and design specification,
    96, 105–107
  obsolescence, 105, 107
  reclamation of materials, 105–106
  and spare part storage, 105
  toxic materials, 106–107
Distribution, effective, as design discipline, 117
Documentation
  in design process, 55
  and design specification, 96

Economies of scale, 125
Energy consumption, 127
  and design specification, 95
Engineering industries, and ending of static
    plateau, 23
Environmental considerations for design
    specification, 88–89
Ergonomics, 115–116
  and design specification, 92
Expert systems, 129–131

Failure of products
  cost recovery, 66–67
  reasons, 11–12
Fashion, as dynamic discipline, 115
Features analysis, 102
Feilden Report, 102
Financial control in design, 64–65, 66–67
Finish of product and status, 115
Forecasting
  life cycle curve in, 38–39
  product status in, 42–43
  S-shaped curve in, 39–42
Front-end bias, 6

Group technology, and product status, 118–119

Health and Safety at Work etc. Act (1974), 28
  see also Safety considerations in design
    specification

Imitation, and product status, 30, 118
Infrastructure of the market, and product status,
  25–26
Innovation seeking for project success, 74–75
Installation, and design specification, 95
Internal combustion engine
  diesel engine design effort, 28
  infrastructure resists change, 25–26

Just in time (Kanban), 127–128

Legal aspects of specification, 94
Legislation, 28
  safety, 94
Life cycle curve, 38–39
  versus S-shaped curve, 41–42
Life of product, and specification
  in production, 91
  in service, 89
  in storage, 93

Machinery
  BS 5740 on, 28
  dedicated, and product status, 31
Maintenance considerations
  as design discipline, 116
  in design specification, 89
Management commitment
  as essential preliminary, 64, 65–66
  and product status, 32–33
Management of design, 6-7, 64–131
  and design specification, 84–107
    contents, 87–96
    element grading, 102–105
    features analysis in, 102
    guidelines for preparation, 96–97
    inadequacies, 86
    parametric analysis in, 98–102
    product status and, 29–30, 97
  need for, 9–16
    company survival, 9–10
    costs and stage of design, 12–16
    customer selection, 9
    failure/success, 11–12
  preliminary layer, 64–67
    financial control, 64–65, 66–67
    management commitment, 64, 65–66
  product definition, 68–71
    sources of design, 69–71
  and product status, 108–121
    dynamic disciplines, 113–114
    and dynamic product, 108–110
    and low-cost production, 114
    and production volume, 112–113
    questionnaire advantages, 80–81

Management of design (cont.)
    questionnaires, 76–81, 82, 142, 143, 153–157
    specification, 72–75
    static 1 disciplines, 114–121
    static 2 disciplines, 122–131
    and static product, 110–112
  worked example, 135–152
    design disciplines and status, 145–148
    design specification, 144–145
    product definition, 135, 137–139
    static 2, 148–150
    status determination, 144
    status specification, 139–144
Market constraints, and design specification, 95
Market pull, 69, 70
Market research, and product status, 72, 73–75
  quality of, 34–35
Market share, 129
  and static product design, 24
Marketing, 7–8
  in design plan, 55–56
  niche, 124–125
Materials
  and design specification, 91
  and product status, 121
  toxic, disposal, 106–107

Niche marketing, 124–125
Nuclear power stations disposal, 106–107

Obsolescence, built in, 105, 107

Packing in design specification, 90
Parametric analysis, 98–102
Patents
  and design specification, 89–90, 95
  as dynamic discipline, 114
Performance function, 18–19
Performance of product, in design specification,
  88
Plant, dedicated, and product status, 31
Process design, 119–121
  and design specification, 90
  dominance, and product status, 33
  in product development, 37
  see also Total design process
Processess, manufacturing, and design
    specification, 93
Product champions, 63
Product definition
  in design process, 68–71
  Sinclair C5 example, 153–157
  worked example, 135, 137–139
Product design specification (PDS), see Design
    specification
Product life cycle (PLC), 38–39
Product status, 6, 17–43
  advantages of knowing, 23–24
  ascertainment in design process, 79–80
  company size and, 81–83
  concept development, 17–19

Product status (*cont.*)
  and cost of design, 66
  curves, 41–42
  design disciplines and, 108–121
    dynamic disciplines, 113–114
    and dynamic product, 108–110
    and low-cost production, 114
    and production volume, 112–113
    and research, non-product-related, 113
    static 1 disciplines, 114–121
    static 2 disciplines, 122–131
    and static product, 110–112
    worked example, 145–148
  and design specification, 97
  factors in, 24–36
    for dynamic product, 25
    macrofactors, 25–29
    microfactors, 29–36
    for static product, 24–25
  for forecasting/prediction, 42–43
  and life cycle, 38–39
  need to detect change in, 20–23
    product examples, 21–22
  performance function and, 18–19
  questionnaires, 76–80
    advantages, 80–81
    for periodic checks, 81
  the S-shaped curve, 39–42
  specification, 72–75
  in typical product development, 36–38
  worked example
    determination, 144
    specification, 139–144

Quality, and design specification, 92
Quality circles, 52
  see also Design circles
Questionnaires, product status, 76–81
  advantages, 80–81
  paper clip example, 142–143
  for periodic checks, 81, 82
  Sinclair C5 example, 153–157

Rationalization, 125
  and product status, 33
Recycling of materials, and design specification,
    105–106
Reliability, and design specification, 92–93
Reputation as design discipline, 116–117
Robots, 31

S-shaped curves, 39–42
Safety considerations in design specification, 94
  see also Health and safety at Work etc. Act
    (1974)
Sales potential, and design specification, 95
Sensitivity analysis, 129

Shelf life specification, 93
Sinclair C5, 153–157
  destined to fail, 22
Size of product
  reduction, and status, 116
  in specification, 91
Slide rule/calculators and product status change,
    22
Spare-part storage costs, 105
Specialization by workers, 126–127
Specification, *see* Design specification
Standards
  as design discipline, 117
  and design specification, 91–92
  and product status, 26
  see also British Standards
Status, *see* Product status
Stockholding costs, 105
Subcontractors
  component supply, and product status, 30–31
  limitations of customer requirements, 35–36
  for manufacture of dynamic products, 113–114

Technology push, 69–71
Test considerations, and design specification, 93
Time for design
  and design specification, 93
  and product status, 32
Tooling, dedicated, and product status, 31
Total design process, 47–63
  activity model, 48, 51, 52
  advantages, 47–48
  communication in, 62–63
  documentation, 55
  marketing in, 55–56
  in organic/mechanistic systems, 61–62
  plan, 48, 49, 50, 58–59
  product champions, 63
  production quantity determination, 56–58
  reviews, 59–60
  team, 52–55
Toxic materials, disposal considerations, 106–107
Training
  for customers, for dynamic products, 113
  of user, and design specification, 95

Value analysis, 128
Venture groups, 63
Videorecording machines
  and status change, 22
  VHS system static plateau, 26
Volvo and group technology, 118

Warehouse costs, 105
Watches, clockwork/electronic, and status change
    in, 21
Weight of product, and specification, 91